First published in 2007 by

Appletree Press Ltd
The Old Potato Station
14 Howard Street South
Belfast BT7 1AP

Tel: +44 (028) 90 24 30 74
Fax: +44 (028) 90 24 67 56
Email: reception@appletree.ie
Web: www.appletree.ie

A catalogue record for this book is available from the British Library.

Great Irish Lives

ISBN: 978 1 84758 001 6

Desk and Marketing Editor: Jean Brown
Copy-editor: Jim Black
Editorial Assistant: Laura Armstrong
Designer: Stuart Wilkinson
Production Manager: Paul McAvoy

Great Irish Lives

Martin Wallace

Introduction

What do I mean by an 'Irish life'? St Patrick was not an Irishman, but no collection of Irish lives would be complete without him. And if he can get in, there is also room for Charles Bianconi, who began life as a very Italian Carlo and went on to revolutionise road transport in Ireland. Some who sought and found fame elsewhere could hardly get away quickly enough – yet their Irishness never left them. Most of the men and women in this book were not only born in Ireland, but spent most of their lives there.

They are a disparate lot, and some are more famous than others. I confess to a particular regard for the Anglo-Irish, for all their faults, a company which includes Edmund Burke and Charles Stewart Parnell merits W.B. Yeats' tag as 'one of the great stocks of Europe'. Among the native Irish patriots and statesmen, I admire most such pragmatists as Daniel O'Connell, Michael Collins and Sean Lemass. I also warm to industrious scholars such as John O'Donovan and Douglas Hyde, who helped to preserve Irish language and tradition, and to awaken an interest in Ireland's past. There are also a few rogues and vagabonds, for no impression of Ireland would be complete without them.

The lives are arranged chronologically, by date of birth. As a footnote to many of the lives, I have noted things and places to see and visit. Samuel Johnson once said that the Giant's Causeway in Co. Antrim was worth seeing, but not worth going to see. **Visit**, in my footnotes, is a recommendation to go and see, and to spend some time. **See** may indicate nothing more than a statue or a house exterior, worth a look if you are in the vicinity. I have listed some important dates overleaf, and there is an Index covering each of my lives, both its main entry and any other life where the person is mentioned.

Dates in Irish History

432	St Patrick's mission to Ireland
795	Viking raids on Ireland begin
1014	Battle of Clontarf
1169	Norman invasion of Ireland
1494	Poynings' Law
1591	Trinity College, Dublin, founded
1601	Battle of Kinsale
1607	Flight of the Earls
1609	Plantation of Ulster
1641	Irish rebellion
1649	Oliver Cromwell in Ireland
1690	Battle of the Boyne
1691	Treaty of Limerick
1695	Penal laws against Catholics
1782	Irish parliamentary independence
1791	Society of United Irishmen founded
1792-93	Catholic Relief Acts
1795	Orange Order founded
1798	United Irishmen's rising
1800	Acts of Union
1803	Robert Emmet's rising
1829	Catholic emancipation
1845-49	Potato famine
1848	Young Irelanders' rising
1858	Irish Republican Brotherhood founded
1867	Fenian rising
1879	Land war begins
1886	Home Rule Bill defeated
1891	Death of Charles Stewart Parnell
1893	Second Home Rule Bill defeated
1904	Abbey Theatre opened
1905	Sinn Féin founded
1912	Ulster Covenant signed
1916	Easter Rising in Dublin
1918	Sinn Féin election successes

1919	First Dáil, War of Independence
1920	Government of Ireland Act – Partition
1921	Truce, Anglo-Irish Treaty
1922	Irish Free State established
1922-3	Civil War
1937	New Irish constitution
1949	Republic of Ireland established
1972	Northern Ireland parliament suspended
1985	Anglo-Irish Agreement
1998	Good Friday Agreement
1999	David Trimble and John Hume win Nobel Peace Prize
2002	Euro becomes currency of Republic of Ireland
2005	IRA declare arms 'beyond use'

Slemish Mountain, Co. Antrim

SAINT PATRICK
c. 390-461
IRELAND'S PATRON SAINT

St Patrick, probably born towards the end of the fourth century, was the son of a minor functionary in Roman Britain. At sixteen, he was captured by Irish raiders and sold to a chieftain, Milchu, whose animals he herded on Slemish Mountain, Co. Antrim. Six years later, he escaped to southern Ireland and sailed on a ship carrying a cargo of wolfhounds to France.

In captivity, Patrick had turned to God, and in dreams had been told to escape; later, he had a vision in which the Irish people called him to return. One tradition suggests he became a disciple of Germanus at Auxerre, in France, and that he set out to convert the Irish after the death of Palladius, whom the Pope had sent to Ireland in 431. His arrival as bishop is commonly dated at 432, his first church being a barn given by Dichu, a local chief, at Saul, Co. Down.

Armagh became his headquarters, and is still the ecclesiastical capital of Ireland. He travelled widely, baptising converts, ordaining bishops and fostering monastic life. His early captivity had equipped him to preach in Irish, and the Roman Church conquered Ireland as the Roman legions had never done.

There are many legends about St Patrick: that he banished snakes from Ireland; that he used the three-leaved shamrock to demonstrate the Holy Trinity; that he lit a Paschal fire on the Hill of Slane, Co. Meath, challenging the pagan flame on nearby Tara. Of the writings attributed to him, only his *Confession* and *Letter to Coroticus* are confidently accepted as his work.

Irish annals generally date Patrick's death at 493, but 461 is also recorded, which fits better with Palladius' known death. He is commonly believed to have died at Saul.

Visit
Croagh Patrick, Co. Mayo (6 miles/9.5 km WSW of Westport) and Lough Derg, Co. Donegal (5 miles/8 km N of Pettigo) attract pilgrims.

See
At Saul, replica of an early church and round tower.
At St Patrick's Cathedral, Downpatrick, a granite block marks the supposed grave of Saints Patrick, Brigid and Colmcille.

SAINT COLMCILLE
521-597
FOUNDER OF MONASTERIES

St Colmcille was born on 7 December 521 in Gartan, Co. Donegal. He was descended from Niall of the Nine Hostages, the high king and forebear of the Ulster O'Neills. He was baptised Colm (and is also known as Columba, the Latin 'dove'), *cille* ('of the church') being added later.

As a chief's son, he was fostered out – but, unusually, to a priest – and later studied at the monastic schools of Moville Abbey, Co. Down, and Clonard, Co. Meath. A seventh-century biographer describes him praying successfully at Moville for spring water to be turned into communion wine; later writers also ascribed miracles to him. The episcopal church of St Patrick had become dominated by monastic settlements, and Colmcille founded his first monastery at Derry in 546. Thereafter, he travelled throughout Ireland, establishing many new settlements, the most notable was Durrow Abbey, Co. Offaly, renowned for its scholarship and illuminated manuscripts.

In 563, Colmcille and twelve followers sailed to the Scottish island of Iona, and founded a monastery which remained the inspiration of Celtic Christianity until the Viking raids of the eighth century. According to tradition, Colmcille had secretly copied a psalter belonging to St Finnian of Moville; Finnian discovered this and claimed the copy. In an early copyright adjudication, the high king Diarmuid ruled 'To every cow her calf, and to every book its copy.'

When Diarmuid killed a youth to whom Colmcille had given sanctuary, the imperious priest persuaded his Uí Néill kinsmen to wage war on the high king. The Uí Néill won the battle of Cuildreimhne, Co. Sligo, in 561, but Colmcille was shocked by the numbers slain. A synod of saints at Tailte, Co. Meath, charged him to convert an equal number of pagans, and Colmcille chose exile to work among the Pictish tribes of Scotland. He played a statesman's role in the growth of the Scottish kingdom of Dalriada, and died in Iona on 9 June 597.

Visit
Columban sites at Durrow Abbey (4½ miles/7 km NE of Tullamore, Co. Offaly),
Moone (2½ miles/4 km S of Ballitore, Co. Kildare) and Glencolumbkille, Co. Donegal.

SAINT COLUMBANUS
c. 543-615
MISSIONARY TO EUROPE

Little is reliably known of St Columbanus' early life, but he was probably born *c.* 543 in Leinster. He left home as a youth to study at Cleenish, Co. Fermanagh, and then entered the monastery at Bangor, Co. Down, founded by St Comgall. He felt a call to missionary work abroad, and *c.* 589 he and twelve followers sailed for Europe.

He is thought to have landed in France near St Malo, and after preaching in the region was summoned to the court of the Frankish king of Burgundy, Gunthram, or possibly Childebert II. Columbanus was allowed to settle in the mountainous wilderness of the Vosges, and he built a monastery at Anegray. According to legend, Columbanus found his own retreat in a bear's den; a holy well marks where he brought water from the barren rock. A second monastery, at nearby Luxeuil, became famous for scholarship. When a third was opened at Fontaine, Columbanus drew up his *Regula Monachorum*, a strict monastic code emphasising obedience 'even unto death', poverty and mortification through fasting.

There were differences between the Celtic and Roman Churches – as in the dating of Easter, the Irish practice of private confession and penance, even the manner of shaving a monk's head – and Columbanus came into conflict with local bishops. In 610, the Irish monks were expelled by Theuderich II. Reaching Nantes, the elderly saint was ready to return to Ireland, but storms persuaded him and his enemies that it was God's intention that he remain.

Eventually, Columbanus arrived at Metz, where King Theudebert invited him to preach to the pagan tribes of central Europe. He settled at Breganz, on the shore of Lake Constance, but when the king was defeated by Theuderich in 612, Columbanus had to move to Lombardy. King Agilulf offered him land at Bobbio, in the Apennines, and he built a new monastery. He died there on 23 November 615, having sent a deathbed message of forgiveness to his last Irish companion Gall, who had refused to leave Lake Constance. St Gall had already celebrated mass for Columbanus, having learned of his death in a vision.

BRIAN BORU
c. 940-1014
HIGH KING OF IRELAND

Reputed burial place of Brian Boru

Brian was born *c.* 940 in north Munster, the youngest son of Cennétig, king of the Dál Cais. In 976, he succeeded his murdered brother Mahon or Mathgamain, and claimed the kingship of Munster. Since 800, the Vikings or Norsemen had founded ports around Ireland, and their longboats easily penetrated Munster. Brian was the first Irish ruler to assemble a fleet to defend and extend his territory. From his seat at Kincora (now Killaloe, Co. Clare), near Lough Derg, he was able to sail up the Shannon to ravage Connacht, Meath and Breifne.

Brian's main Irish rival was Malachy, king of Meath, who had become high king at Tara in 980. Malachy had driven the Viking Olaf out of Dublin; Olaf's son, Sitric, eventually ruled

Dublin under Malachy. In 997, the two kings agreed to divide Ireland between them, Brian gaining suzerainty over Dublin. In 999, the Leinstermen joined with Sitric against Brian, only to suffer defeat at Glenmama, Co. Wicklow.

Brian married Gormflath (who had been married successively to Olaf and Malachy), gave his own daughter to Sitric, and claimed the northern half of Ireland. Malachy failed to marshal the support of the Northern Uí Néill, and in 1002 conceded the high kingship. Collecting tribute and hostages on his royal journeys, Brian acquired the name Boru (Brian of the Tributes). In 1005, he gave twenty ounces of gold to the Church, and recognised the archbishop of Armagh as primate of all Ireland.

In 1013, the unfaithful Gormflath roused Sitric and her brother Maelmora, king of Leinster, against Malachy. Brian came to Malachy's aid, but failed to take Dublin and retired to Kincora. Sitric made an alliance with Sigurd, earl of Orkney, who delivered 2,000 Norse soldiers and was promised Gormflath in marriage. The Leinstermen and Vikings were routed at Clontarf, outside Dublin, on 23 April 1014, but the aged Brian was slain in his tent. His death foreshadowed new dynastic conflicts which left Ireland vulnerable to the Norman invasion in 1169.

See

A tablet in the outer wall of the north transept of St Patrick's Church of Ireland Cathedral marks Brian's reputed grave.

SAINT MALACHY
1094-1148
CHURCH REFORMER

St Malachy was the son of a renowned teacher in Armagh and was probably born there in 1094. A devout and studious boy, he attached himself to a hermit, Imar, and so impressed the archbishop of Armagh, Cellach, that he made him his vicar. He was ordained in 1119, and soon showed reforming zeal in establishing the Roman liturgy and in such matters as confession, confirmation and marriage rites.

Stained glass impressions of St Malachy

Abuses were now prevalent in the Celtic Church. In monasteries, the post of abbot was often handed down within a family; some abbots were laymen, some were married. Reformers saw the need to enforce higher standards through a strong central organisation wielding authority derived from Rome. In 1121, Malachy went to Lismore, Co. Waterford, to study under Malchus, a bishop knowledgeable about Church organisation.

In 1123, Malachy became abbot of Bangor, Co. Down, rebuilding the monastery which Vikings had destroyed, and in 1124 bishop of Down and Connor. In 1129, the dying Cellach named Malachy as his successor, breaking the hereditary tradition. A usurper claimed the archbishopric, and Malachy was not consecrated until 1132, nor did he enter Armagh until

1134. Having restored peace and discipline, he resigned in 1137 and founded an Augustinian priory at Downpatrick, Co. Down.

In 1139, Malachy set out for Rome to seek from the Pope the symbolic *pallium* or lambswool collar for the archbishops of Armagh and Cashel. On his journey, he was so impressed by the abbey of Clairvaux, in France, that he left four companions to train in the austere Cistercian discipline. In 1142, Mellifont Abbey became the first of thirty-nine Cistercian foundations in Ireland, an incursion which, with other reforms and the Anglo-Norman invasion, signalled the end of the Celtic Church.

In 1148, Malachy set out again for Rome. He was in poor health, and died at Clairvaux on 2 November 1148.

Visit
Cistercian remains at Mellifont Abbey (5 miles/8 km NW of Drogheda, Co. Louth),
Boyle Abbey (Boyle, Co. Roscommon) and Jerpoint Abbey (1 mile/1.5 km SW of Thomastown, Co. Kilkenny).

See
A plaque marks the saint's reputed birthplace in Ogle Street, Armagh.

GARRET MORE FITZGERALD
EARL OF KILDARE
c. 1456-1513
KING'S DEPUTY

Gerald Fitzgerald, whom the Irish called Garret More, was probably born in Maynooth Castle, Co. Kildare, *c.* 1456. At the time, there were three great Anglo-Irish families. The Geraldines or Fitzgeralds of Leinster (earls of Kildare) and of

Munster (earls of Desmond) supported the House of York in England's Wars of the Roses. The Butlers (earls of Ormond) supported Lancaster. When Garret More became eighth Earl of Kildare in 1478, his family enjoyed a pre-eminence which he maintained for a further half-century.

In the absence of a king's deputy, he was soon elected caretaker 'justiciar' by the Irish Council (the deputy's advisers and ministers), and resisted King Edward IV's attempt to install an English deputy. He sailed to England and was confirmed as deputy. Judicious marriage alliances, linking Old English lords and Gaelic chiefs, extended his influence.

In 1485, the Lancastrian Henry VII became king. Two years later, Kildare supported Lambert Simnel, a pretender who was crowned in Dublin, but an invasion of England failed. Kildare was pardoned, but came under suspicion when another pretender, Perkin Warbeck, landed at Cork in 1491. A new deputy, Edward Poynings, arrived in 1492. Poynings' parliament of 1494-5 accused Kildare of treason, and he was imprisoned in the Tower of London. The so-called Poynings' Law subordinated the hitherto independent Irish parliament to the king.

Henry VII restored Kildare as deputy in 1496, reputedly saying, 'Since all Ireland cannot rule this man, this man must rule Ireland.' In 1504, the 'Great Earl' defeated his son-in-law, Ulick Burke of Clanrickard at Knockdoe, Co. Galway, in the first Irish battle employing firearms. On 3 September 1513, Kildare himself was killed by a musket during a skirmish with the O'Mores of Laois. The new deputy was his son, Garret Oge, but Poynings' Law already foreshadowed a centralised monarchy, and a new conquest of Ireland would soon mark the end of the Gaelic lordships and the native culture which had flourished under Kildare.

See

Remains of Maynooth Castle, at the entrance to St Patrick's College, Maynooth, Co. Kildare.

GRACE O'MALLEY
c. 1530- *c.* 1603
PIRATE QUEEN

Grace O'Malley was born *c.* 1530 in Co. Mayo. Among many variants of her name, Gráinne Ni Mhaílle is common; she is also called Granuaile or Gráinne Mhaol (Grace of the cropped hair), having adopted a boy's haircut to sail to Spain on her father's ship. He was Owen 'Black Oak' O'Malley, chieftain of the lands around Clew Bay. The O'Malleys were noted seafarers, engaging in piracy as well as trading and fishing.

Rockfleet Castle, Co. Mayo

Grace married another pirate, Donal O'Flaherty, *c.* 1546. His family ruled Iar-Connacht and Connemara; Galway city's west gate was inscribed 'From the ferocious O'Flaherties good Lord deliver us'. Donal is thought to have died in battle with the Joyces after seizing a castle on Lough Corrib. He was known as Donal the Cock, and the fortress was named Hen's Castle after Grace's subsequent spirited defence.

For a time, Grace made Clare Island the headquarters of her piracy, but in 1566 she married Richard Burke, whose Rockfleet Castle guarded a safe harbour on the north of Clew Bay. One legend suggests she dissolved the marriage as he returned from a voyage, but held the castle. More probably, she dominated him until his death in 1583; the lord deputy, Sir

Henry Sidney, called her 'a notorious woman in all the coasts of Ireland' when the couple submitted to him at Galway in 1577.

In 1593, Grace petitioned Queen Elizabeth for liberty 'to invade with sword and fire all your highness' enemies', and sailed up the Thames to meet the Queen at Greenwich. Her suit was apparently successful, but the governor of Connacht, Sir Richard Bingham, considered her 'a notable traitress and nurse of all rebellions in the province for forty years' and continued to harass her until he left Connacht in 1595. Little is known of her last years but her lands were plundered and she is thought to have died in poverty c. 1603.

See
Well-preserved castles associated with Grace O'Malley include:
Rockfleet (3 miles/4.5 km W of Newport, Co. Mayo),
Kildawnet Castle on Achill Island and one on Clare Island.

HUGH O'NEILL,
EARL OF TYRONE
1550-1616
SOLDIER AND GAELIC LEADER

O'Neill was born at Dungannon, Co. Tyrone, in 1550, entering a Gaelic world of tribal rivalry, passion and intrigue. His father was Matthew O'Neill, 1st Baron Dungannon and illegitimate son of Conn O'Neill, Earl of Tyrone and 'The O'Neill'. Matthew's claim to the earlship was disputed by his half-brother, Shane O'Neill, who procured his murder. When Conn died in 1559 and Shane became The O'Neill, Hugh was taken into the protection of the Queen's deputy, Sir Henry Sidney, and raised as an English nobleman. In 1567, Shane was succeeded by his son, Turlough.

In 1568, Hugh finally settled in Ulster. Initially loyal

to Queen Elizabeth, he led a troop of horse against the Desmond rebellion of 1569, and in 1573 assisted the 1st Earl of Essex in an attempted colonisation of Co. Antrim. In 1587, he was formally granted the earldom of Tyrone, and in 1593 he supplanted the ailing Turlough as The O'Neill. He was now able to unite the Irish chiefs in defence of Gaelic life, law and tradition.

The Blackwater River

In 1595, O'Neill destroyed an English fort near the present Blackwatertown, Co. Armagh. He then defeated an expedition led by Sir Henry Bagenal, his brother-in-law, at Clontibret, Co. Monaghan. In 1598, O'Neill exploited the boggy Ulster terrain to achieve the greatest Irish victory over an English army, when he defeated and slew Bagenal at the Yellow Ford near Blackwatertown. The English plantation of Munster was swept away.

In 1599, the 2nd Earl of Essex arrived with an army, but only managed to negotiate a truce; he was replaced by Lord Mountjoy. O'Neill had long sought Spanish aid, and in 1601 more than 3,000 Spanish soldiers landed at Kinsale, Co. Cork, where they were besieged by Mountjoy. O'Neill abandoned caution, marched to Kinsale, and was routed in a pitched battle. He retreated to Ulster, eventually surrendering in 1603.

In 1607, O'Neill led the 'Flight of the Earls', sailing from Lough Swilly to exile in Europe with more than ninety Gaelic chiefs. He died in Rome on 20 July 1616.

GEOFFREY KEATING
c. 1570- *c.* 1650
POET AND HISTORIAN

Geoffrey Keating (or Seathrún Céitinn) was born *c.* 1570 in Burges, Co. Tipperary. Of Anglo-Norman stock, he was educated at a local bardic school, and then at Bordeaux, in France, where he studied for the Catholic priesthood. He returned to Ireland *c.* 1610 as a doctor of theology, and served in different parishes near his birthplace. His popularity as a preacher grew steadily, but after a sermon directed against the mistress of a local squire he had to take refuge in a cave in the Glen of Aherlow.

While in hiding, he began his famous *History of Ireland* or *Foras Feasa ar Éirinn* (literally 'a basis of knowledge about Ireland'), travelling widely to consult manuscripts held in great houses. It was begun in 1629, and completed by the time he emerged as a parish priest in Cappoquin, Co. Waterford, in 1634. He returned to Tubrid, near his birthplace, *c.*1644 and erected a mortuary chapel in which he is buried. He may have died in that year, but one tradition is that he was murdered in nearby Clonmel by Oliver Cromwell's soldiers in 1650.

Keating's major work was the first cohesive history of Ireland written in the Irish language, and it was a counter balance to the works of English authors such as Edmund Spenser and Giraldus Cambrensis. Copies of the manuscript were widely circulated, but the book was not printed in Irish until the twentieth century; English translations were published early in the eighteenth century. A patriotic history, it helped to preserve the myths and sagas of Gaelic Ireland on which its author uncritically drew.

Keating was also a poet, writing both in the formal bardic style of syllabic verse and in the new stressed verse of the seventeenth century, which was to achieve a wider popularity. Some poems are lyrical; others are patriotic, the new verse

proving well suited to impassioned laments for lost heroes and braver times. He also wrote several works of theology, and his *Three Shafts of Death* or *Trí Biorghaoithe an Bháis* is an urbane and scholarly collection of anecdotes, arguments and pieties.

See
Keating's vestments are in the museum of St Patrick's College, Maynooth, Co. Kildare.

MÍCHEÁL Ó CLÉIRIGH
c. 1575-1643
SCHOLAR AND ANNALIST

Ó Cléirigh (Michael O'Clery) was born at Kilbarron, overlooking Donegal Bay. His date of birth is commonly given as 1575, but may have been earlier. Baptised Tadgh, he became Brother Mícheál on entering the Franciscan order at the Irish College at Louvain, in Belgium.

Donegal Bay

In 1626, he returned to Ireland, joining the Franciscan convent at Bundrowes, near Bundoran, Co. Donegal. His mission was to collect material for a work on the lives of Irish saints, *Acta Sanctorum Hiberniae*, planned by Father Hugh Ward, professor of theology at Louvain, and carried on by his successor, Father John Colgan. Many ancient manuscripts had been destroyed in Irish wars, and Ó Cléirigh's laboriously compiled copies helped to preserve at Louvain much of the historical record that remained at risk. He also began to assemble his own calendar of Irish saints, commonly known as *The Martyrology of Donegal*.

With three other historians, Ó Cléirigh travelled to the convent of Killinure, on the shore of Lough Ree, where they compiled *Réimh Ríoghraidhe na hÉireann agus Seanchas na Naomh* (The Succession of the Kings and the Genealogies of the Saints of Ireland). In 1631, they moved to the convent of Lisgoole, overlooking Lough Erne, to begin revising the *Leabhar Gabhála*, the *Book of the Invasions of Ireland*.

On 22 January 1632, Ó Cléirigh and his three assistants began the *Annála Rioghachta Éireann* (Annals of the Kingdom of Ireland). They were to become famous under the title used by Colgan, *The Annals of the Four Masters*. The work was completed at Bundrowes on 10 August 1636, and chronicled Irish history from early times to the early seventeenth century. The *Annals* were austerely written, and detailed such major events as wars and raids, the burning and rebuilding of monasteries, the crowning and death of kings; written in Irish, they were translated by John O'Donovan in the nineteenth century. In 1637, Ó Cléirigh returned to Louvain, where he died in 1643.

OWEN ROE O'NEILL
c. 1590-1649
SOLDIER

O'Neill's date of birth has traditionally been given as *c.* 1590, but it may have been several years earlier. His father was Art O'Neill, younger brother of Hugh O'Neill. Educated in Spain,

O'Neill served that country as a professional soldier. He formed his own regiment, and in 1640 won praise for a gallant defence of Arras; he finally negotiated an honourable surrender to his French opponent, who acknowledged that O'Neill had 'surpassed us in all things save good fortune'.

Benburb Castle, Co. Tyrone

When the Irish rebellion of 1641 broke out, O'Neill secured his release from the Spanish army and arrived in Lough Swilly in July 1642. He joined up with Sir Phelim O'Neill, his cousin and instigator of the rebellion, and became general of the Ulster Catholic forces.

The Anglo-Normans or Old English joined the native Irish in the Catholic 'Confederation of Kilkenny', favouring Charles I as his dispute with the English parliament turned into civil war. O'Neill took the confederacy oath in November 1642, receiving supplies to fight the parliamentary army led by the Scottish general, Robert Monro. The Old English had always inclined towards a political settlement with the king's deputy, the Earl of Ormond, but the native Irish wanted to uproot the Protestant planters in Ulster and regain confiscated land. O'Neill was encouraged by the papal nuncio, Cardinal Rinuccini, and in 1646 heavily defeated Monro at Benburb, Co. Tyrone. It was the first Irish victory in a formal pitched battle, but O'Neill failed to consolidate his success.

Rinuccini rejected a peace offer from Ormond which the Old English favoured. O'Neill later abandoned a siege of Dublin after disagreeing with Thomas Preston, the confederacy's inept commander in Leinster. Ormond then surrendered Dublin to parliamentary forces, which inflicted defeats on Preston and on the confederate army in Munster.

The arrival of Oliver Cromwell in August 1649 persuaded O'Neill to a new defence of his religion. On his way to join a royalist army assembled by Ormond, he died at Cloughoughter Castle in Lough Oughter, Co. Cavan, on 6 November 1649.

SAINT OLIVER PLUNKETT
1625-1681
ARCHBISHOP AND MARTYR

Plunkett (or Plunket) was born into an influential Anglo-Norman family on 1 November 1625 at Loughcrew, near Oldcastle, Co. Meath. In 1647, he travelled to the Irish College in Rome, and was ordained a priest in 1654. To avoid Cromwellian persecution, Plunkett petitioned to remain in Rome, and in 1657 became a professor of theology.

In time anti-Catholicism eased, and in 1669 Plunkett was appointed archbishop of Armagh. He set about reorganising the ravaged Church, and built schools both for the young and for clergy whom he found 'ignorant in moral theology and controversies'. He tackled drunkenness among the clergy, writing 'Let us remove this defect from an Irish priest, and he will be a saint.'

In 1670, he summoned an episcopal conference in Dublin, and later held numerous synods in his own archdiocese. However, he had a long standing difference with the archbishop of Dublin, Peter Talbot, over their rival claims to be primate of Ireland. He also antagonised the Franciscans, particularly when he favoured the Dominicans in a property dispute.

With the onset of new persecution in 1673, Plunkett went into hiding for a time, refusing a government edict to register at a seaport and await passage into exile. In 1678, the so-called Popish Plot concocted in England by Titus Oates led to further anti-Catholicism. Talbot was arrested, and Plunkett again went into hiding; the privy council in London was told he had plotted a French invasion.

In December 1679, Plunkett was imprisoned in Dublin Castle, where he gave absolution to the dying Talbot. Taken to London, he was found guilty in June 1681 of high treason, largely on perjured evidence from two disaffected Franciscans. On 1 July 1681, Plunkett became the last Catholic martyr in England when he was hanged, drawn and quartered at Tyburn. He was beatified in 1920 and canonised in 1975, the first new Irish saint for almost seven hundred years.

See

Plunkett's head is preserved in a shrine at St Peter's Church, West Street, Drogheda, Co. Louth.

TURLOUGH CAROLAN
1670-1738
HARPER

Carolan (or O'Carolan) was born in 1670 near Nobber, Co. Meath. His family moved to Co. Roscommon, where his father worked for the MacDermott Roe family of Alderford, near Ballyfarnon. When at eighteen he lost his sight from smallpox, Mrs Mary MacDermott Roe arranged tuition in the harp, and later provided a horse and servant for his travels.

Music-making was a common occupation for the blind, and Carolan was well received in great houses. He was most renowned as a composer, and repaid hospitality by naming tunes after his benefactors – with titles such as 'Planxty Reynolds', 'Planxty Maguire', the planxty being a tune for the harp, and 'Bumper Squire Jones'. An early love affair inspired the tune 'Bridget Cruise'; years later, he recognised the touch of her fingers when climbing into a ferryboat during a pilgrimage to Lough Derg, Co. Donegal.

Carolan became a friend of Dr Patrick Delany, professor of oratory at Trinity College, Dublin, and through him of Jonathan Swift; Delany translated an Irish verse for which Carolan had written the melody. Italian music was popular in the city, and Carolan was influenced by Corelli, Vivaldi and Geminiani.

He travelled mainly in Ulster and Connacht, and his wife came from Co. Fermanagh. They built a small house near Mohill, Co. Leitrim, and had seven children. Her death inspired one of his laments. When Carolan himself felt death near, he returned to Alderford and played his 'Farewell to Music'. According to one story, he was unable to drink a cup of whiskey, so kissed the cup, saying that such old friends should not part without a kiss. He died on 25 March 1738, and was buried in the MacDermott Roe family chapel at Kilronan Abbey. He was the last of the great Irish harpers, who vanished as the traditional Gaelic culture yielded to the penal laws.

See
Kilronan graveyard (2½ miles/4 km SE of Ballyfarnon, on the Sligo-Drumshanbo road).
Carolan's harp at Clonalis House, near Castlerea, Co. Roscommon.
Memorial in St Patrick's Cathedral, Patrick Street, Dublin.

AODHAGÁN Ó RATHAILLE
c. 1670-c. 1726
BARD

Aodhagán Ó Rathaille (or Egan O'Rahilly) was born c. 670 in the rugged Sliabh Luachra district of Co. Kerry. Little is known of his early life, but he was well versed in Latin and English as well as his native tongue, and may have attended one of the last bardic schools in Killarney. His family were farmers, owing a new allegiance to the Browns, Roman Catholic landlords whose Elizabethan forebears had supplanted the Gaelic MacCarthys.

The defeat of the Jacobite cause at Derry, the Boyne and Aughrim in 1689-91 foreshadowed the penal laws of 1695 onwards. Ó Rathaille reached manhood as a civilisation came to an end. In 1691, following the Treaty of Limerick, Gaelic chiefs left Ireland in large numbers to serve as mercenaries in European armies. The poet or bard was left without a patron. Unlike the harper Carolan (*see page 26*), Ó Rathaille had nothing to offer the Anglo-Irish settlers who replaced the Gaelic lords – though in a poem recalling the past glories of a MacCarthy stronghold, he was careful to flatter the new occupant.

Many of his poems were elegies in which he listed genealogies going back centuries; some were satires. Most enduring are his lyric poems, particularly 'Gile na Gile' (Brightness of Brightness). It is one of his *aisling* or vision poems, and Ireland is represented by a beautiful woman left (in James Clarence Mangan's translation) 'to languish Amid a ruffian horde till the Heroes cross the sea'. The heroes never returned; the Jacobite cause foundered.

Ó Rathaille must have recited at the so-called courts of poetry, occasional gatherings which replaced the bardic schools, and copies of his poems were widely circulated. He was reduced to poverty in later life, recalling in one poem that he had not needed to eat dogfish or periwinkles in his youth. He died in 1726 without leaving his native Munster.

See

Ó Rathaille is buried at Muckross Abbey (2½ miles/4 km S of Killarney). He and three other Kerry poets are commemorated in a monument by Seamus Murphy in College St, Killarney.

GEORGE BERKELEY
1685-1753
PHILOSOPHER AND BISHOP

Berkeley was born in Co. Kilkenny on 12 March 1685. He was educated at Kilkenny College, before entering Trinity College, Dublin, in 1700. He graduated in 1704, and was elected a fellow in 1707. In 1710, he took holy orders, as was required of fellows.

Trinity College was then more progressive than Oxford or Cambridge universities, and John Locke's *Essay on Human Understanding* (1690) had quickly become part of the philosophy course. Berkeley's study of Locke, and the contradictions he detected, led him to become an 'immaterialist', denying the existence of matter and arguing that things depended for their existence on being perceived: *esse est percipi* (to be is to be perceived). Among several works which established a European reputation was his masterpiece, *A Treatise concerning the Principles of Human Knowledge* (1710).

Granted leave in 1713, he quickly made a mark in London's drawing-rooms and coffee-houses, enjoying the friendship of Swift, Pope, Addison and Steele. He travelled widely in France and Italy before returning to Dublin in 1721.

In 1724, he was appointed Dean of Derry, and launched an ambitious project for a college in Bermuda. 'Westward the Course of Empire takes its Way' he wrote in a poem; he hoped to prepare colonists' sons for the ministry and to educate young American Indians. He sailed for the New World in 1728, but returned to England in 1731 when a promised government grant failed to materialise. In *Alciphron* (1732), he defended Anglican Christianity against free thinkers.

In 1734, Berkeley became bishop of Cloyne, Co. Cork. In *The Querist* (three volumes, 1735-7), he posed almost six hundred cogent questions about social and economic conditions in Ireland. He became an advocate of 'tar-water', describing the resinous medicine as 'so mild and benign and proportioned to the human condition, as to warm without heating, to cheer but not inebriate'. Ill, he resigned in 1752 and died in Oxford on 14 January 1753. Alexander Pope had already paid tribute in a poem: 'To Berkeley, every Virtue under Heav'n'.

See
Memorial in the thirteenth-century St Colman's cathedral at Cloyne.

PEG WOFFINGTON
c. 1718-1760
ACTRESS

Margaret Woffington was born in Dublin, possibly on 18 October 1718. A pretty child, Peg sold watercress in the street, where she was recruited into Madame Violante's company of juveniles, performing in a booth in George's Lane. At twelve, she played Polly Peachum in *The Beggar's Opera*. In 1732, she accompanied Violante to London, playing Macheath at the Haymarket, but returned to Dublin when the venture failed.

Peg was next apprenticed to the famous Smock Alley theatre, under Francis Elrington. He opened a new Theatre Royal in Aungier Street, and she soon became a leading performer. When she played Sylvia in Farquhar's *The Recruiting Officer*, her success in soldier's uniform set a pattern for many future performances. Her greatest role in breeches, which displayed her fine figure, was Sir Harry Wildair in Farquhar's *The Constant Couple*. 'I have played the part so often that half the town believes me to be a real man,' she once confided to an actor, James Quin, who replied 'Madame, the other half knows you to be a woman'.

In 1740, Peg took London by storm, repeating at Covent Garden her roles in Farquhar's comedies. The following year, Mrs Woffington (as she was now billed) played Cordelia at Drury Lane. Lear was played by a new young actor, David Garrick. After a summer season at Smock Alley, they returned to London as lovers, but parted in 1744. Their professional relationship also soured, and in 1748 Peg moved to Covent Garden.

In 1751, Peg returned to Smock Alley, now managed by Thomas Sheridan, godson of Swift and father of Richard Brinsley Sheridan; when he founded the Beefsteak Club for his influential patrons, Peg became president. In 1754, she returned successfully to Covent Garden, where a feud with the actress George Anne Bellamy once caused Peg to drive her rival off the stage. In declining health, she collapsed on stage in 1757 while playing Rosalind in *As You Like It*. It was her last performance, and she died on 28 March 1760. She was buried at Teddington, where she had lived and had endowed alms-houses.

ARTHUR GUINNESS
1725-1803
BREWER

Guinness was born in Celbridge, Co. Kildare, in 1725. His father was land steward to the Archbishop of Cashel, Dr Arthur Price, and brewed beer for workers on the estate. When Price died in 1752, he left £100 each to the two Guinnesses, which may have encouraged the young man to lease a brewery in Leixlip, Co. Kildare, in 1756. Three years later, he left this brewery in charge of a younger brother, and took over one at St James's Gate in Dublin.

He began by brewing beer or ale, and within eight years was master of the Dublin Corporation of Brewers. In 1761 he married Olivia Whitmore, a relative of Henry Grattan, and ten of their twenty-one children lived to establish a dynasty which has spread into many activities and countries. The family's long association with St Patrick's Cathedral began with a gift of 250 guineas for the chapel schools, and Dublin enjoyed other benefactions.

St James's Gate, Dublin

There was, however, one dispute with Dublin Corporation, whose investigators concluded that Guinness was drawing more free water than his lease permitted. In 1775, the brewer seized a pickaxe to defend his supplies from the sheriff, and eventually reached a peaceful solution after protracted litigation. Duties on beer proved another problem, and in 1795 Guinness enlisted Grattan's oratory to persuade the government to remove the burden.

In 1778, Guinness began to brew porter – the darker beer containing roasted barley and first drunk by London porters – and exploited Ireland's new canals to extend his market. In 1799, he brewed ale for the last time. Sales of porter increased threefold during the Napoleonic Wars, and in time St James's Gate became the largest porter and stout brewery in the world, its 'extra stout porter' becoming known simply as stout.

Guinness gradually handed over control to three sons, and spent his last years at Beaumont, his country home in Drumcondra, now a Dublin suburb. He died on 23 January 1803.

Visit
Guinness Store House, St James's Gate, Dublin 8.

EDMUND BURKE
1729-1797
PHILOSOPHER AND POLITICIAN

Burke was born at 12 Arran Quay, Dublin, probably on 1 January 1729. The son of a prosperous Protestant attorney and Catholic mother, he graduated from Trinity College, Dublin, in 1748, and studied law at the Middle Temple, in London. However, his interests were literary, and in 1759 he became first editor of the *Annual Register*, an immediately influential world review.

Burke statue at Trinity College

In 1757, Burke married Jane Nugent of Bath, a Catholic who thereafter embraced Anglicanism. He entered Westminster in 1766 as MP for the 'rotten borough' of Wendover, and held this and other seats until 1794. Although he proved a forceful if indiscreet orator, his diffuseness in later years earned him the nickname 'Dinner Bell'. Burke raised the level of political debate by arguing from moral principle rather than expediency, articulated the role of MP as representative rather than delegate, fostered the party system, and did much to abolish corrupting sinecures. His precarious finances and lack of practical judgement tarnished his own reputation, however, and he was denied high office. 'Though equal to all things, for all things unfit,' wrote his friend Oliver Goldsmith.

Every major political problem engaged Burke. He championed individual liberty against the monarchy, urged conciliation of the American colonists before the War of Independence, and in 1786 moved the impeachment of Warren Hastings, former governor-general of India. His European reputation rested on *Reflections on the Revolution in France* (1790), Burke foreseeing a threat to the ordered liberty of England. His conservative ideas split the Whigs, ended a long friendship with Charles James Fox, and evoked a famous reply in Tom Paine's *Rights of Man*.

In 1794, Burke was succeeded as MP for Malton by his son Richard, whom he expected to become chief secretary in a reforming Irish administration under Lord Fitzwilliam. His son died of consumption, however, the tactless Fitzwilliam was recalled, and as in America the stage was set for revolution. A disappointed Burke died on 9 July 1797.

See
Statue by John Henry Foley in Trinity College, Dublin.

FREDERICK HERVEY,
EARL OF BRISTOL
1730-1803
BISHOP

Hervey was born at Ickworth, the family seat in Suffolk, on 1 August 1730. Educated at Westminster School and Cambridge University, he took holy orders in 1755. In 1766, his brother George, 2nd Earl of Bristol became Lord Lieutenant of Ireland. Frederick acted as his chaplain, and was soon appointed Bishop of Cloyne, Co. Cork. In 1768, playing leapfrog, he learned that he had gained the more profitable bishopric of Derry, and declared 'Gentlemen, I have surpassed you all. I have jumped from Cloyne to Derry.'

Hervey built two great houses in his new diocese: Downhill, overlooking Lough Foyle, and the unfinished Ballyscullion, at nearby Lough Beg. His third was a reconstruction of Ickworth, which his wife (who left him in 1782) considered 'a stupendous monument to folly'. He introduced church reforms, added spires to make churches more visible, and pressed for an easing of the penal laws against Roman Catholics. He succeeded to the earldom in 1779.

The threat of French invasion led to the formation of companies of Volunteers, an armed militia which strengthened the political and economic demands of the emerging 'Protestant nation'. As colonel of the Derry Volunteers, the Earl Bishop was feted on his way to the 1783 convention of Volunteers in Dublin. However, a deception by Sir Boyle Roche thwarted his hopes of committing the movement to Catholic emancipation.

A great traveller, Hervey filled his houses with Italian and Flemish art treasures; another interest was geology, stimulated when an arm was injured during an eruption of Vesuvius. Many European hotels were named after him, and in his later years he was seldom in Ireland. Always an eccentric, he openly associated with courtesans such as Lady Hamilton and Countess Lichtenau. Once when a woman of easy virtue entered Lady Hamilton's salon, he retired saying it was permissible for a bishop to visit a sinner but not to be seen in a brothel. He died near Rome on 8 July 1803.

Visit

Mussenden Temple (National Trust), near Downhill ruins (1 mile/1.5 km W of Castlerock, Co. Londonderry), named after a female cousin.

SIR BOYLE ROCHE
1743-1807
POLITICIAN

Roche, member of an old Anglo-Norman family, was born in 1743. Having served with distinction in the army, he became MP for Tralee in 1776. He held this and other seats until the Acts of Union in 1800, and his consistent support of the government gained him a baronetcy in 1782. He was also chamberlain to the vice-regal court.

During the 1783 convention of Volunteers in Dublin, the Earl of Bristol, Bishop Hervey, argued for extending the franchise to Roman Catholics. An opponent of emancipation, George Ogle, produced a letter denying that Catholics sought further concessions, and Roche confirmed that he had received it from a leading Catholic, Lord Kenmare. The convention consequently took no action, even though it later emerged that Roche had lied. Unperturbed, Roche explained that he had 'resolved on a bold stroke…authorised only by a knowledge of the sentiments of the persons in question'. It was his most notable political act, but he is better remembered as the perpetrator of Irish 'bulls'.

It was not unusual for members of the government to write Roche's speeches, which he committed to memory. While he usually retained the substance of a speech, he inclined towards verbal contradictions or 'bulls'. Best recalled, perhaps, is 'Mr Speaker, I smell a rat; I see him forming in the air and darkening the sky; but I'll nip him in the bud.' He once asked 'How could I be in two places at once unless I were a bird?' and insisted that 'Half the lies our opponents tell about us are untrue.' Attributed to him are 'What has posterity done for us?' and 'All along the untrodden paths of the future I can see the footprints of an unseen hand.'

Roche was an active supporter of the Union, declaring that his love for England and Ireland was such that he would have the two sister nations embracing like one brother. However, he spoke prophetically when he warned that 'The cup of Ireland's miseries has been overflowing for centuries, and is not yet full.' Roche died at his home at 63 Eccles Street, Dublin, on 5 June 1807.

HENRY GRATTAN
1746-1820
POLITICIAN

Grattan was born on 4 July 1746. His father was recorder of Dublin for many years; his mother was daughter of a chief justice. He graduated from Trinity College, Dublin, in 1767 and was admitted to the Middle Temple in London to study law. He spent much of his time at Westminster, admiring the oratory of Edmund Burke, and his landlady complained of him walking in the garden at night addressing an invisible 'Mr Speaker'.

Statue at College Green

He was called to the Irish Bar in 1772, and in 1775 entered the parliament in Dublin as MP for the borough of Charlemont, Co. Armagh. Grattan quickly supplanted Henry Flood as leader of the 'patriot party', and in 1779 persuaded the British government to remove most of the restrictions on Irish trade; he was aided by the rise of a Protestant militia, the Volunteers. In

1782, Westminster conceded Grattan's demand for Irish parliamentary independence, and grateful MPs voted him £50,000, which he unwisely accepted.

Flood undermined Grattan's leadership by insisting further assurances of Irish independence were needed, and Westminster conceded the 1783 Act of Renunciation. It proved worthless and impaired the unity of the 'Protestant nation'. The two rivals had to be restrained from fighting a duel. 'Grattan's Parliament' coincided with the flowering of Georgian Dublin. There was some easing of the penal laws, for he believed that 'the Irish Protestant should never be free until the Irish Catholic ceased to be a slave', but in 1795 the recall of the reforming lord lieutenant, Lord Fitzwilliam, ended the prospect of further change. Ill, and opposed to both the government and the revolutionary United Irishmen, Grattan retired from parliament in 1797. He returned in 1800, and in Volunteer uniform spoke against the proposed Union with Great Britain. In 1805, encouraged by Fitzwilliam and Charles James Fox, Grattan entered Westminster, but he was unsuccessful in his battle for Catholic emancipation. He died in London on 4 June 1820, and was buried in Westminster Abbey.

See
Statue by John Henry Foley at College Green, Dublin.

BRIAN MERRIMAN
c. 1747-1805
POET

Merriman (in some Irish manuscripts, Brian MacGiolla Meidhre) was born c. 1747, probably near Ennistymon, Co. Clare. He may have been a farmer's son, educated at a hedge school or by a priest, and he was an accomplished fiddler. By 1770, he had become a teacher at Feakle, Co. Clare, then a poor and isolated area. He also farmed twenty acres, and won prizes from the Dublin Society for growing flax. He was almost forty when he married.

Merriman's fame rests on a single poem in Irish of 1,206 lines, *Cúirt an Mheán Oíche* or *The Midnight Court*, written c. 1780. It was widely circulated in manuscript during his life, and published in Dublin towards the end of the century as *Media Noctis Consilium*. The poem has attracted many translators, among them Percy Arland Ussher, Frank O'Connor, the 6th Earl of Longford and Thomas Kinsella. Apart from two lyrics attributed to him, *The Midnight Court* is all that has survived of Merriman's work. No one knows if he wrote anything else; certainly, he lived far from the courts of poetry which survived in Co. Kerry and which might have encouraged him.

In the poem, the author is walking by Lough Graney when he is summoned to stand trial at a fairy court in nearby Feakle, where he is accused of remaining a bachelor. A lyrical opening soon gives way to the bawdy comedy of the trial, covering such subjects as promiscuity, illegitimacy, impotence and the celibacy of clergy. Finally, the poet is stripped for punishment by the assembled women – and then wakes up. Merriman's humour often recalls his Scottish contemporary, Robert Burns; long after his death, he was to trouble the Irish Censorship Board.

Late in life, Merriman moved to the city of Limerick, where he died on 27 July 1805. One of the few certainties about his life is the entry in the *General Advertiser and Limerick Gazette*: 'Died on Saturday morning, in Old Clarestreet, after a few hours' illness, Mr Bryan Merryman, teacher of Mathematics, etc'.

See

A plaque marks the old graveyard in Feakle where Merriman is buried; his grave has not been identified.

JOHN PHILPOT CURRAN
1750-1817
BARRISTER

Curran was born on 24 July 1750 in Newmarket, Co. Cork. At first intended for the Church, he was deflected by the dissipations of student life in Dublin and opted instead for the Irish Bar. His wife's small dowry helped him withstand early poverty; when she ran off with a clergyman in 1793, a subsequent court case exposed Curran's own infidelities.

Despite a shrill voice and stutter, his career flourished on the notorious Munster Circuit, where corruption prevailed. In 1780, he represented a Catholic priest who had been horsewhipped by Lord Doneraile. Curran's fame was assured when his eloquence moved a Protestant jury to award the priest damages. He became a King's Counsel 1782, and entered parliament the following year. Among his causes were penal reform, alleviation of peasant poverty, and Catholic emancipation.

In 1785, he fought a duel with the attorney-general John Fitzgibbon, and his chancery practice declined after the latter became lord chancellor in 1789. Curran prospered in other courts, and was seldom bettered for witty insult. A rival, 'Bully' Egan, threatened to put the tiny Curran in his pocket. 'If you do that,' came the reply, 'you'll have more law in your pocket than you ever had in your head.'

A judge afflicted with ague brought the remark 'You may have observed his lordship shaking his head while I have been speaking, but I can assure you, gentlemen of the jury, that there is nothing in it'. Curran's most famous saying was entirely serious, when he warned 'The condition upon which God hath given liberty to man is eternal vigilance'.

Curran defended several United Irishmen before and after the 1798 rising. However, following the fiasco of the 1803 rising, he refused to represent Robert Emmet, who had courted his daughter Sarah; Curran had to protest his own innocence of treason. In 1806, Curran was appointed master of the Irish rolls. He retired in 1814, and died at Brompton, Middlesex, on 14 October 1817.

See
Bust in St Patrick's Church of Ireland Cathedral, Dublin.

RICHARD MARTIN
1754-1834
POLITICIAN

Martin was born in February 1754. His family was one of the powerful 'tribes of Galway', and his father had lately turned Protestant to secure his lands. Educated at Harrow and Cambridge University, Martin was MP for Jamestown, Co. Leitrim, from 1776 to 1783. Called to the Irish Bar in 1781, he appeared in only one case, representing Charles Fitzgerald against his brother George 'Fighting' Fitzgerald, who had shot a wolfhound, and with whom Martin later fought several duels. He then became a magistrate, commanded the Galway Volunteers, and was commonly called 'King of Connemara'.

Ballynahinch Castle

His first wife was Elizabeth Vesey, who infatuated Wolfe Tone when he tutored Martin's stepbrothers and joined in the family's amateur theatricals, and later left her husband for another man. Beset with debts Martin took refuge in Ballynahinch Castle, an inaccessible house in Connemara. On his father's death in 1794, he inherited an estate covering one-third of Co. Galway, and in 1796 married Harriet Evans, author of *Historic Tales* and later of a novel, *Helen of Glenross*. He returned to parliament in 1798 as MP for Lanesborough, Co. Leitrim, supported the Union with Great Britain, and entered Westminster in 1801 as MP for Co. Galway.

Martin was disappointed in his efforts to remove the death penalty for forgery, and to allow prisoners accused of capital crimes to be represented by counsel. However, he had a memorable success in 1822, when his Ill-Treatment of Cattle Bill became the first British measure for animal protection. In 1824, he was a founder of the (now Royal) Society for the Prevention of Cruelty to Animals, and he was noted for his readiness to defend any passing animal against a cruel master. The Prince Regent (later George IV) nicknamed him 'Humanity Dick'.

Martin was unseated by petition after an election victory in 1826, and escaped his creditors by settling in Boulogne, in France, where he died on 6 January 1834. A year later, his Act was extended to cover cruelty to all animals.

EDMUND IGNATIUS RICE
1762-1844
EDUCATIONIST

Rice was born on 1 June 1762 at Westcourt, near Callan, Co. Kilkenny. His father was an unusually prosperous Roman Catholic farmer, and the son was sent at fourteen to complete his education in Kilkenny. At sixteen, he was apprenticed to his uncle, a merchant and ships' chandler in Waterford. Rice was always a devout Catholic and, when his wife died in 1789, he gave increasing time and thought to his faith.

A capable businessman, he inherited his uncle's business in 1794. Drawn into charitable works, he helped to house the destitute and alleviate prison conditions. In 1802, he opened a boys' school in a stable in New Street Waterford. He soon retired from business and, joined by two young volunteers from Callan, lived austerely in a loft.

Rice next built a monastery, Mount Sion, on the outskirts of Waterford, setting up a bake-house to feed hungry pupils. Additional schools were opened at nearby Carrick on-Suir in 1806 and Dungarvan in 1808. Rice and his companions followed rules adapted from Presentation nuns and, assuming monk's dress, became Brother Ignatius.

New schools were opened in Cork, Dublin and else where, and in 1817 Rice sought papal approval for a constitution under which all the foundations would be amalgamated under a superior-general. Not all the Catholic bishops welcomed this, but in 1822 he was elected superior-general of the Irish Christian Brothers. The brothers were to devote their lives to the free religious and literary instruction of boys, especially the poor, and were bound by vows of obedience, chastity, poverty and perseverance.

The first English school was opened at Preston in 1825. When Rice retired in 1838, the order had seventeen houses and forty-three schools, and this remarkable institution continued to spread through many parts of the world. Rice died at Mount Sion on 29 August 1844.

Visit

Rice's home, carefully restored, near Callan. Mausoleum at Mount Sion, Waterford, with memorial chapel.

See

Statue of Rice by Peter Grant in Main St, Callan.

THEOBALD WOLFE TONE
1763-1798
REVOLUTIONARY

Tone was born at 44 Stafford Street (now Wolfe Tone Street), Dublin, on 20 June 1763. Educated at Trinity College, Dublin, he was called to the Bar in 1789, but was more interested in politics. When Tone published *An Argument on behalf of the Catholics of Ireland* under the pseudonym 'A Northern Whig', he was invited to Belfast to assist in founding the Society of United Irishmen, which met first on 18 October 1791. A Dublin society was soon formed, but Tone was associated more with the

United Irishmen sculpture in Castlebar, Co. Mayo

Catholic Committee, whose paid agent he became in 1792.

In 1794, an eccentric cleric, William Jackson, arrived in Ireland to assess for the French government the likely success of an invasion. Tone unwisely wrote a memorandum for him; when Jackson was betrayed and arrested, Tone was fortunate to escape arrest. He was allowed to emigrate to America in 1795. As he later wrote, he sought to break the connection with England, and 'to substitute the common name of Irishman, in place of the denominations of Protestant, Catholic and Dissenter': in Belfast he joined with United Irishmen in an oath to this end.

The French minister in Philadelphia encouraged Tone to

take his invasion plan to revolutionary France. An invasion fleet left Brest in December 1796, but bad weather prevented a landing. Tone persuaded the French into new expeditions, but by the time Gen. Humbert landed in Co. Mayo in August 1798, the United Irishmen's rising in Ulster and Leinster had failed. Humbert was soon defeated, and Tone was captured aboard a French ship in Lough Swilly, Co. Donegal, on 12 October. He admitted treason and, when his request to be shot as a soldier was refused, he cut his own throat in Dublin on 12 November, dying in prison on 19 November 1798.

Visit
Kilmainham Jail Museum, Dublin.

See
Plaque in Wolfe Tone Street, and memorial by Edward Delaney in St Stephen's Green, Dublin. Republican memorial at Bodenstown (1 mile/1.5 km N of Kill, Co. Kildare), where Tone is buried.

LORD EDWARD FITZGERALD
1763-1798
REVOLUTIONARY

Fitzgerald was born on 15 October 1763. He was the twelfth child of James Fitzgerald, 20th Earl of Kildare, and his wife, daughter of the Duke of Richmond. The earl became 1st Duke of Leinster in 1766, but died in 1773. A year later, his widow married their son's tutor, William Ogilvie, and they lived in France until 1779. Returning to England, Fitzgerald joined the army, and was wounded at Eutaw Springs, in America, in 1781.

In 1783, he returned to Ireland to become MP for Athy, Co. Kildare, supporting Henry Grattan in the Irish parliament.

Unsuccessful romances led him to return to the army. He served in Canada, was adopted into the Bear tribe of Indians in Detroit, and finally journeyed down the Mississippi river. Returning to England, he had an affair with the dying wife of Richard Brinsley Sheridan.

Fitzgerald's burial place

Fitzgerald was friendly with Tom Paine, author of *The Rights of Man*, and in 1792 joined him in Paris. Attending a dinner to celebrate French victories, Fitzgerald toasted the 'speedy abolition of all hereditary titles and feudal distinctions', and was cashiered from the army. He also met and married Pamela Sims, adopted daughter of the novelist and educationist Madame de Genlis and probably her daughter by the Duke of Orleans.

Back in Ireland, Fitzgerald increasingly identified himself with the cause of Irish independence; he wore a green cravat, burned turf rather than English coal, and sang patriotic ballads. Early in 1796, he joined the now illegal United Irishmen, and travelled to the Continent to discuss with Gen. Hoche the possibility of a French invasion. In January 1798, he headed a military committee to plan the imminent rising.

On 12 March 1798, the members of the Leinster Directory were arrested. Fitzgerald had warning and went into hiding, but he was betrayed and arrested in Dublin on 19 May; he killed a militia officer in the struggle, and was himself shot in the shoulder. He died in Newgate prison, Dublin, on 4 June 1798.

See
Plaque in Thomas St, Dublin, where Fitzgerald was arrested.

BUCK WHALEY
1766-1800
RAKE

Thomas Whaley was the son of Richard Chapell Whaley, a Protestant landowner and magistrate whose anti-Catholicism earned him the nickname 'Burn-Chapel' Whaley. When the latter died, his son inherited an estate in Co. Wicklow, a town house at 86 St Stephen's Green, Dublin (now occupied by University College, Dublin), and an income of £7,000 a year. At sixteen, Whaley was sent to Paris, but his tutor was unable to curb the youth's profligacy. Whaley incurred gambling debts of £14,000 in an evening, and was forced to leave France when his bankers refused to honour his cheque.

Back in Dublin, he was asked one evening in 1788 where he next intended to visit. Already known as 'Buck' he acquired his second nickname when he casually replied 'Jerusalem'. His fellow bucks wagered £15,000 that he could not reach the holy city and return within two years. Despite fears of banditry, Whaley immediately launched an expedition to the Holy Land, returning in June 1789 with a signed certificate from a convent in Jerusalem. Another wager required him to jump from his drawing room window into the first passing carriage and kiss its occupant. He also conceived a plan to rescue Louis XVI from the guillotine, but took fright in Paris.

A man of erratic impulses, Whaley unsuccessfully proposed marriage to a young Belfast woman who stood admiring his house. A mistress bore him several children, and on her death he married Lord Cloncurry's daughter in 1800. He represented Newcastle, Co. Dublin, in parliament from 1785 to 1790, and Enniscorthy, Co. Wexford, from 1797 to 1800. Although he took substantial bribes first to vote for the Union with Great Britain and then to vote against it, his financial difficulties forced him to flee to the Isle of Man. To live on Irish soil without being in Ireland (for a bet), he imported earth for the foundations of a new house.

Whaley died of rheumatic fever at Knutsford, Cheshire, on 2 November 1800. In his last years, he had written his memoirs as a warning to others, but his executors suppressed them and they were not published until 1906.

ROBERT STEWART,
VISCOUNT CASTLEREAGH
1769-1822
POLITICIAN

Stewart was born at 28 Henry Street, Dublin, on 18 June 1769. His father was a Presbyterian landowner and MP, who built an imposing home, Mount Stewart, near Newtownards, Co. Down. His mother was the daughter of an English earl, as was his stepmother. Educated at Armagh Royal School and Cambridge University, Stewart was elected MP for Co. Down in 1790.

Although a member of the Northern Whig Club, Stewart leaned towards William Pitt's Tories and a career at Westminster. In 1794, he married Lady Emily Hobart, daughter of the Earl of Buckinghamshire, and became MP for Tregony in Cornwall. In 1795, his step-uncle, the Earl of Camden, became lord lieutenant and Stewart gave up his Westminster seat to join the Irish administration in 1797. His father was now 1st Earl of Londonderry, and Stewart was known by the courtesy title of Viscount Castlereagh.

In March 1798, he became temporary chief secretary through the illness of Thomas Pelham, and was instrumental in the arrest of the United Irishmen's leaders before the 1798 rising. Castlereagh was reviled for the cruelty of the rising's suppression, but his appointment was confirmed in November 1798. In 1800, he secured the passage of the Act of Union in Ireland by unscrupulous bribery and patronage, but resigned over George III's rejection of Catholic emancipation.

Thereafter, Castlereagh pursued his political career at Westminster, becoming secretary for war in 1805 and foreign secretary in 1812. He played a notable diplomatic role in the defeat of Napoleon and in the 1815 Congress of Vienna, but domestic policies later made him as unpopular in England as he was in Ireland. Always cold and aloof, he became increasingly depressive, and on 12 August 1822 cut his throat at his country seat in Kent. His contemporary Byron described him as having cut his country's throat, and Shelley once wrote 'I met Murder on the way – He had a mask like Castlereagh – Very smooth he looked, yet grim; Seven bloodhounds followed him'.

Visit
Mount Stewart (National Trust property, 5 miles/8 km SE of Newtownards, Co. Down).

EDWARD BUNTING
1773-1843
MUSICIAN

Bunting was born in Armagh in 1773. He was the youngest of three sons, all of whom became musicians. The eldest, an organist at Drogheda, Co. Louth, was his first teacher. At eleven, the musical prodigy was articled to the organist of St Anne's Church in Belfast, and became popular as performer and teacher.

Bunting lived with a Presbyterian family, the McCrackens, who were much influenced by revolutionary ideas from

America and France; the son, Henry Joy McCracken, was hanged as a United Irishman in 1798. Henry's uncle, the newspaper proprietor Henry Joy, was one of the promoters of an ambitious harp festival in Belfast in July 1792, coinciding with celebrations commemorating the storming of the Bastille in Paris.

The harpers performed over three days; all but one were old, and the majority blind. Bunting was commissioned to transcribe the music, and his imagination was immediately stirred. He soon set off with the harper Denis Hampson to collect airs in the Magilligan district of Co. Londonderry. When Bunting played an Irish air, 'The Parting of Comrades', at a farewell party for Wolfe Tone in 1795, Tone's wife was reduced to tears.

In 1796, Bunting's pioneering work was published as *A General Collection of the Ancient Irish Music*, with sixty-six airs adapted for the pianoforte. In 1802, he made an extended tour of Connacht and Munster, but now collected the verses accompanying the airs. In 1809, he published a second volume, containing seventy-seven airs, of which twenty had verses translated from the Irish. A year earlier, Thomas Moore had drawn from the 1796 volume the music for eleven of his *Irish Melodies*.

On the formation of the Belfast Harp Society in 1808 Bunting became its musical director, in 1815, he toured Europe extensively, playing Irish music to appreciative audiences. He married in 1819, and moved to Dublin where he became organist of St George's Church in Hardwicke Place. His third volume, *The Ancient Music of Ireland*, was published in 1840. Bunting died in Dublin on 21 December 1843.

DANIEL O'CONNELL
1775-1847
POLITICIAN

O'Connell was born near Cahirciveen, Co. Kerry, on 6 August 1775. Adopted by a childless uncle, Maurice 'Hunting Cap' O'Connell of Derrynane House, overlooking Kenmare Bay, he attended English colleges in France before they were closed by revolutionaries.

The O'Connell family were prosperous Roman Catholics; it had been illegal to educate the boy abroad, but a 1792 Relief Act changed this and also allowed him to become a successful barrister on the Munster Circuit.

O'Connell statue, Dublin

A constitutionalist in politics, O'Connell opposed the violence of the 1798 and 1803 risings, and in 1815 was distressed when he killed an opponent who had forced him into a duel. In 1823, he formed the Catholic Association; membership eventually cost a 'Catholic rent' of a penny a month. His objective was Catholic emancipation, opening up state and judicial posts and the right to sit in parliament. A powerful nationwide organisation quickly emerged, with the help of clergy, and in 1824 the government unsuccessfully prosecuted O'Connell for inciting rebellion.

In 1828, he won a by-election in Co. Clare, but unwillingness to take the anti-Catholic oath of supremacy kept him out of Westminster. The following year, the government conceded Catholic emancipation; 'The Liberator', as he was now known, entered parliament after a by-election. In 1840, O'Connell again marshalled mass support in the National Repeal Association, his oratory drawing enormous crowds. However, in 1843, he accepted a government ban on a rally planned for Clontarf on the outskirts of Dublin, and lost ground to the more militant 'Young Irelanders' under Thomas Davis. In 1844, he was found guilty of creating discontent and disaffection, and was in prison for three months before the House of Lords reversed the judgement. He died in Genoa, on his way to Rome, on 15 May 1847.

Visit
Derrynane House (1½ miles/2km SW of Caherdaniel, Co. Kerry), now a national historic park and museum.

See
Statues in O'Connell Square, Ennis, Co. Clare;
in the Crescent, Limerick; and in O'Connell Street, Dublin.

ROBERT EMMET
1778-1803
REVOLUTIONARY

Emmet was born at 124 St Stephen's Green, Dublin, on 4 March 1778. He was the youngest son of Dr Robert Emmet, physician to the lord lieutenant, and brother of the United Irishman Thomas Addis Emmet. He entered Trinity College in 1793, joined the United Irishmen soon afterwards, and was consequently expelled from college in February 1798.

Thomas Addis Emmet was arrested in March 1798, released in 1802, and lived in Paris before emigrating to America in 1804. Robert, now a wanted man, sought his brother's advice about a new rising, and met the French leaders, Bonaparte and Talleyrand. Deciding he could not rely on French aid, he returned secretly to Dublin in October 1802.

Thomas Russell, friend of Wolfe Tone and recently released from Fort George, undertook to lead the rising in Ulster. Emmet established arms dumps in Dublin and with Russell tested an explosive rocket at Rathfarnham. On the evening of 23 July 1803, he donned a green uniform and led a hundred followers towards Dublin Castle. On the way, they stopped the carriage of the lord chief justice Lord Kilwarden, and murdered him and his nephew. The rabble were quickly dispersed, however, and Emmet fled to the Wicklow mountains. No Ulster rising occurred.

His love of Sarah Curran, daughter of prominent legal figure John Philpot Curran, kept him from escaping to France, and he was discovered in hiding at Harold's Cross. The fiasco of Emmet's rising was redeemed by his famous speech from the dock, ending 'Let no man write my epitaph; for as no man who knows my motives dare now vindicate them, let not prejudice or ignorance asperse them... When my country takes her place among the nations of the earth, then, and not till then, let my epitaph be written.' On 20 September 1803, Emmet was hanged in Thomas Street, Dublin. Russell was betrayed and hanged at Downpatrick, Co. Down, on 21 October 1803.

See
Statue by Jerome Connor facing Emmet's birthplace in St Stephen's Green, Dublin.
Plaque in Thomas St, Dublin.

CHARLES BIANCONI
1786-1875
TRANSPORT PIONEER

Carlo Bianconi was born in northern Italy on 24 September 1786. At fifteen, he was apprenticed to an Italian print-maker who took him to Dublin. Young Charles – as he called himself – was soon tramping the roads to Waterford and Wexford to sell prints, and continued on his own account after his apprenticeship ended. An early friend was Theobald Mathew, who rescued him from a fight, and in Waterford Edmund Rice helped him improve his education. In 1809, Bianconi opened a shop in Clonmel, Co. Tipperary, selling prints and mirrors; he also dealt profitably in gold bullion, reselling peasants' guineas to the government for the Napoleonic wars.

With peace came lower grain prices and reduced demand for horses, and Bianconi saw an opportunity to compete with canals and stagecoaches. He negotiated a contract to carry mail, and on 6 July 1815 the first Bianconi car (a horse-drawn two-wheeler carrying six passengers back-to-back facing the roadside) travelled ten miles from Clonmel to Cahir, Co. Tipperary.

Within a year, 'Bians' were covering more than 21 miles a day, in a network extending from Limerick to Waterford. Within twenty years, the crimson and yellow open cars (in different sizes) were familiar almost everywhere west of a line joining Letterkenny, Co. Donegal, and Wexford. Bianconi became a popular figure among Irish Catholics when, in 1826, his cars brought supporters of Daniel O'Connell to vote in a critical Waterford by-election.

He became a naturalised British subject in 1831, which allowed him to buy land. He was elected Mayor of Clonmel in 1844, and in 1846 bought Longfield, an imposing house near Cashel, Co. Tipperary, which he had coveted since his days as a pedlar. A far-sighted businessman, he refused to join canal owners in *res*isting innovation; instead, he bo... *d re*—routed his Bians to connect with... shares in railways, and... services. A driving acc*iden*t in 1865 persuaded him to beg... selling his coaching em*pire,* and he died at Longfield on 22... September 1875.

HENRY COOKE
1788-1868
CLERIC

Cooke was born at Grillagh, near *Maghe*ra, Co. Derry, on 11 May 1788. The son of a tenant far*mer, he w*as educated locally before entering Glasgow College i*n 1802,* and was ordained a Pres*b*yterian minister in 1808. He *served* at Duneane and then D*o*negore, Co. Antrim; after hi*s marriage* in 1813, his presby*te*ry allowed him to study furt*her in Gla*sgow and in Dublin. In 1818, he was called to Killyle*a*gh, Co. Down.

More *t*han anyone, Cooke led Uls*te*r Presb*y*terianism away from the free-thinking radicalism *which had* spawned the United Irishmen's rising during his chi*l*dhood. He gained prominence i*n* 1821 by routing in debate a *visiting* English preacher, John Smethurst, who held Arian or U*nitarian* views. In 1824, Cook*e* was elected moderator of the Synod of Ulster.

By 1829, his oratorical command over the synod was such that the Arians, led by his rival Henry Montgomery, were forced to withdraw. In the same year, Cooke was called to a new church in May Street, Belfast, where he drew large congregations. In 1836, the synod made subscription to the Westminster Confession of Faith obligatory, and in 1840 it merged with the even more conservative Secession Synod to form the General Assembly of the Presbyterian Church in Ireland. Cooke was elected moderator in 1841 and again in 1862.

In defeating the Arians, Cooke had deliberately expelled political liberals; Montgomery's elder brothers had fought as United Irishmen. In 1834, Cooke addressed a mass rally of Protestants at Hillsborough, Co. Down, forging a new alliance between Presbyterians and the established Church of Ireland to defend their interests against the newly emancipated Catholics. When Daniel O'Connell visited Belfast in 1841, Cooke staged a huge anti-Repeal rally.

He opposed the national system of undenominational schooling begun in 1831, and in 1840 won financial aid for Presbyterian schools. He also secured government support for a new Presbyterian College in Belfast, and became its president in 1847. He died in Belfast on 13 December 1868.

See
Statue in College Sq East, Belfast.

FATHER THEOBALD MATHEW
1790-1856
TEMPERANCE CAMPAIGNER

Mathew was born at Thomastown Castle, near Golden, Co. Tipperary, on 10 October 1790. He enrolled in Maynooth College in 1807, but left after a breach of the seminary's rules and entered the Capuchin convent in Church Street, Dublin. He was ordained in 1814.

After a brief period in Kilkenny, Father Mathew was sent to the 'Little Friary' in Blackamoor Lane, Cork, where he won a reputation as preacher and sympathetic confessor. He opened a school for girls, and founded a society whose young men worked among the poor and sick. In 1822, Mathew was elected provincial of the Irish Capuchins, holding office until 1851.

Temperance societies had grown up to combat the evils of alcohol among the Catholic poor, and Mathew was

Rosse became president of the Royal Society from 1848 to 1854, was a member of the Royal Irish Academy, and was chancellor of Dublin University from 1862 until his death at Monkstown, Co. Dublin, on 31 October 1867. His son Laurence also became an eminent astronomer.

Visit
In 1997 Rosse's telescope was restored to working order in Birr Castle demesne, where a small museum records his achievement. Nearby is a small suspension bridge which he designed.

SIR WILLIAM ROWAN HAMILTON
1805-1865
MATHEMATICIAN

Hamilton, a solicitor's son, was born at 36 Lower Dominick Street (now demolished), Dublin, on 4 August 1805. At seven, he could read Hebrew, at twelve, he had a knowledge of Arabic, Hindustani, Malay, Persian and Sanskrit, in addition to more common languages. These were encouraged with a view to a clerkship in the East India Company, but Hamilton revealed greater precocity in mathematics, and at seventeen had detected an error of reasoning in Pierre Laplace's classic *Mécanique Céleste*. The Irish astronomer royal, Dr John Brinkley, soon pronounced him 'the first mathematician of his age'.

In 1824, during his second year at Trinity College Dublin, he read a paper to the Royal Irish Academy, and was encouraged to develop this into a 'Theory of System of Rays' (1828), which on theoretical grounds predicted conical refraction. He was still an undergraduate when in 1827 he was appointed professor of astronomy at Trinity College and astronomer royal at Dunsink observatory, Finglas, Dublin. He was knighted in 1835, became president of the Royal Irish Academy in 1837, and was the first foreign member of the National Academy of Sciences in America.

Hamilton received gold medals from the Royal Society for his work on optics and dynamics. He later concentrated on pure mathematics, and in 1844 defined the 'quaternions' which were to form the basis of his new calculus. His system was published in 1853, and had applications in solid geometry, physics, astronomy, crystallography, electrodynamics and other studies involving movement in three dimensional space. A fellow mathematician compared the quaternion to an elephant's trunk, 'ready at any moment to do anything, be it to pick up a crumb or a field gun, to strangle a tiger, or uproot a tree'.

Throughout his life, Hamilton read widely in the many languages at his command. He also wrote poetry, and numbered William Wordsworth and Maria Edgeworth among his friends. He died in Dublin on 2 September 1865.

See
Plaque on the Royal Canal bridge at Broombridge Road, Dublin, where in a 'flash of genius' in 1843 Hamilton scratched on the stonework the formula for quaternion multiplication.

JOHN O'DONOVAN
1809-1861
GAELIC SCHOLAR

O'Donovan was born on 25 July 1809 at Atateemore, Co. Kilkenny. His father was a farmer who, on his deathbed, repeated several times to his son their line of descent from a third-century king of Munster. In 1826, O'Donovan joined the Irish Record Office, working on Irish manuscripts and law documents. In 1829, he was appointed to the historical department of the Ordnance Survey of Ireland; he worked initially on place-names for maps but later, under the antiquarian George Petrie, collected historical material for the proposed memoirs to accompany the maps. His letters were later edited by Father Michael O'Flanagan as *The John O'Donovan Archaeological Survey* (fifty volumes, 1924-32).

O'Donovan also wrote for *The Dublin Penny Journal* and *The Irish Penny Journal*, notably a valuable series on Irish family names. In 1840, he and his brother-in-law Eugene O'Curry helped to found the Irish Archaeological Society, which published much of his best work. He was a prolific scholar, translating many early manuscripts. In 1845, *A Grammar of the Irish Language* compared medieval and modern modes of spoken and written Irish.

His greatest work of translation was the *Annals of the Four Masters*, compiled by Mícheál Ó Cléirigh. It was published in seven volumes (1848-51), with original text and translation on facing pages. With O'Curry, who in 1854 became professor of archaeology and Irish history in the new Catholic University, O'Donovan opened up new worlds of learning, encouraging the study of Irish history and providing materials to inspire the writers and artists of the Celtic Revival.

After his Ordnance Survey work ended in 1842, he studied law and was admitted to the Irish Bar in 1847. In 1849, he became professor of Celtic languages at Queen's College, Belfast, but had no students. In 1852, he joined the Brehon Law Commission, formed to publish the *Seanchus Mór* or ancient laws of Ireland, but did not live to complete this monumental work. He died of rheumatic fever in Dublin on 9 December 1861.

See

Plaque at O'Donovan's home, 36 Upper Buckingham St, Dublin.

THOMAS DAVIS
1814-1845
AUTHOR AND PATRIOT

Davis was born at Mallow, Co. Cork, on 14 October 1814, shortly after the death of his father, an army surgeon. In 1818, his mother and four children moved to Dublin, settling at 61 (now 67) Lower Baggot Street, where they remained together until Davis's death. He graduated from Trinity College, Dublin, in 1836 and was called to the Bar a year later. He joined the National Repeal Association founded by Daniel O'Connell and in 1840 made a notable speech at Trinity's historical society, pleading for studies of Irish history.

In 1841, Davis and his college friend John Blake Dillon, a barrister, met a young journalist called Charles Gavan Duffy. Duffy shared their burgeoning allegiance to Irish nationhood and independence, and while walking in Phoenix Park they planned a newspaper. Davis was a Protestant, the others were Roman Catholics, and under Duffy's editorship they published *The Nation*. The first weekly issue appeared on 15 October 1842, with the slogan 'Educate that you may be free'.

Readership soon reached 250,000, outstripping ever other Dublin journal. Davis found he could write stirring patriotic ballads such as 'A Nation Once Again' and 'The West's Asleep'. *The Nation* also published John Kells Ingram's 'Who Fears to Speak of '98?', and in 1843 the best songs were published as *The Spirit of the Nation*. Davis also launched *The Library of Ireland* (1845-7), a monthly series of shilling volumes in which his own essays and poems were to influence later patriots.

He and his associates, known as 'Young Irelanders' grew increasingly impatient with O'Connell. Davis found the Repeal Association's approach too sectarian; he favoured the undenominational education proposed in the 1845 Colleges

Bill, while O'Connell spoke of 'godless education'. What is unknown is whether or not Davis would have supported John Mitchel and other Young Irelanders as they moved towards rebellion in 1848, for he died at home of fever on 16 September 1845.

See
Plaques at his birthplace, now 72 Thomas Davis St, Mallow, and at his Dublin home. Statue in Mount Jerome cemetery, Dublin. Memorial by Edward Delaney in College Green, Dublin.

JOHN MITCHEL
1815-1875
REVOLUTIONARY

Mitchel was born on 3 November 1815 at Camnish, near Dungiven, Co. Londonderry. The son of a Unitarian minister and United Irishman, he was educated at Trinity College, Dublin, before entering a solicitor's office in Newry, Co. Down. He later practised in Banbridge, Co. Down. In 1836, he eloped to England with sixteen-year-old Jane Verner, but was brought back in custody; they eloped again in 1837 and were married.

Mitchel began writing for *The Nation,* and when Thomas Davis (*see page 62*) died in 1845, Charles Gavan Duffy invited Mitchel to join the newspaper. He subsequently wrote masterly descriptions of the potato famine, contributed a life of Hugh O'Neill (*see page 19*) to *The Library of Ireland*, and edited the poems of Davis and James Clarence Mangan. In 1846, Mitchel and other Young Irelanders broke with Daniel O'Connell (*see page 51*), rejecting the doctrine of 'moral force', and founded the Irish Confederation.

More impatient than Duffy, Mitchel soon left *The Nation* and the Confederation, and in February 1848 published the first issue of *The United Irishman*. It openly preached sedition to 'that numerous and respectable class of the community, the men of no property', and in May 1848 Mitchel was convicted of treason felony and sentenced to fourteen years' transportation. He hoped his sentence would provoke an insurrection, but nothing more than a skirmish in Co. Tipperary ensued.

Sent to Van Diemen's Land (now Tasmania), Mitchel escaped in 1853 to America, where he published his famous *Jail Journal*. In one entry, he welcomes the Crimean War, believing an Irish rebellion can succeed only if England is preoccupied elsewhere. The sentiment influenced Patrick Pearse (*see page 100*) in 1916.

Mitchel launched several newspapers in America, and as editor of the *Richmond Examiner* championed slavery; he was imprisoned for several months after the Civil War ended. In 1867, he founded the *Irish Citizen* in New York, but angered Fenians by suggesting they should give allegiance to their new country. In 1875, he was returned unopposed as MP for Tipperary, but was disqualified as a convicted felon. Returning to Ireland, he was again elected, but died at Dromalane, Newry, on 20 March 1875 before he could be unseated.

VERE FOSTER
1819-1900
EDUCATIONIST AND PHILANTHROPIST

Foster was born on 26 April 1819 in Copenhagen, where his Anglo-Irish father was British minister. He was a great grandson of Frederick Hervey; his grandmother Elizabeth Foster (*née* Hervey) became mistress and later wife of the 5th Duke of Devonshire. Foster also joined the diplomatic service, holding posts in South America during 1842–47.

In 1847, he visited the family estates in Co. Louth during the potato famine, and in 1849 toured more distressed counties with his brother Frederick. He determined to become an enlightened landlord, and trained for a year at the Glasnevin model farm outside Dublin. Concluding that Ireland was overpopulated, he financed forty emigrants to America. In 1850, he himself experienced the abuses and cruelties of an emigrant ship; his description of the voyage led to remedial legislation.

In 1852, Foster established an Irish Female Emigration Fund, proposing that beneficiaries 'of good character' should repay the grants by sending for or assisting relatives in Ireland. Controversy attended his good works when some girls ended up in New York brothels. At home, the loss of cheap labour was sometimes resented, while priests suspected him of proselytism.

Foster turned to improving school accommodation in Ireland, and used his own money to rebuild hundreds of primitive schoolhouses. His philanthropy was particularly appreciated by ill-paid teachers, for whom he provided housing, and in 1868 he became first president of the Irish National Teachers' Association. His other great educational work was to devise the very successful 'Vere Foster Copy Books' to improve schoolchildren's writing. The printing was eventually taken over by a Belfast firm, and in 1867 Foster settled in the city.

He renewed his interest in emigration, and in all helped some 25,000 people to leave Ireland. He also edited *The Two Duchesses* (1898), using family correspondence to recount the unusual friendship between his grandmother and Georgiana, Duchess of Devonshire. A bachelor, he died in Belfast on 21 December 1900, his fortune reduced to £178.

JAMES STEPHENS
1824-1901
REVOLUTIONARY

Stephens was born in 1824 in Kilkenny, where his father was an auctioneer's clerk. Little is known of his early life, but at twenty he was working on construction of the Limerick and Waterford railway. With famine gripping Ireland, he was influenced by the revolutionary ideas of John Mitchel, and began drilling secretly with a few intimates.

In July 1848, he joined in the abortive Young Ireland rising, bravely but inadequately led by William Smith O'Brien, which began and ended with a skirmish with police at Ballingarry, Co. Tipperary. Wounded in the thigh, Stephens escaped to Paris with Michael Doheny, who later described their adventures in *The Felon's Track* (1849); in Kilkenny, Stephens' friends pretended he had died, and buried a stone-filled coffin. In Paris, Stephens earned a living through teaching and journalism but also plotted revolution with John O'Mahony, another survivor of Ballingarry.

O'Mahony and Doheny eventually sailed to America, and in 1856 Stephens tramped through Ireland to assess the prospects for a new rising. On 17 March 1858, he founded the secret Irish Republican Brotherhood in Dublin, and with Thomas Luby Clarke began to gather recruits. O'Mahony led the IRB's American counterpart, the Fenian Brotherhood.

In 1861, the death of another Ballingarry survivor, Terence Bellew McManus, allowed Stephens to stage an impressive funeral at Glasnevin cemetery in Dublin. In 1863, he launched a republican newspaper, *The Irish People*, and later promised the Irish Americans that 1865 would be 'the year of action' though he knew the movement was badly armed. The rising was scheduled for 20 September, the anniversary of the execution of Robert Emmet, but the plot was betrayed and his offices raided.

Stephens avoided arrest until November, then escaped from Richmond jail. Finding himself distrusted by the American Fenians, he fled to Paris and took no part in the unsuccessful 1867 rising. He was allowed to return to Ireland in 1891, and lived at Blackrock, Co. Dublin. He died on 29 April 1901.

WILLIAM EDWARD HARTPOLE LECKY
1838-1903
HISTORIAN and POLITICIAN

Lecky was born into a wealthy property-owning family at Newtown Park, Co. Dublin, on 26 March 1838. Having abandoned early thoughts of taking holy orders, on graduating from Trinity College, Dublin, he travelled widely in Europe, as he was to do throughout his life. His early publications were anonymous and attracted little attention: *Friendship, and Other Poems* (1859), *The Religious Tendencies of the Age* (1860) and *Leaders of Public Opinion in Ireland* (1861).

Lecky statue, Dublin

However his *History of the Rise and Influence of the Spirit of Rationalism in Europe* (1865) brought immediate fame, and the young author found himself much in demand in intellectual circles. The two-volume study traced mankind's gradual discarding of magic and superstition in favour of reason and moral ideas and revealed the breadth of Lecky's reading. Settling in London, Lecky soon completed an equally successful companion piece *History of European Morals from Augustus to Charlemagne* (1869). In 1870 Queen Sophia of the Netherlands asked to meet the historian during a visit to England, and the following year he married her maid of honour, Elisabeth van Dedem.

In 1878 the first two volumes of Lecky's *History of England in the Eighteenth Century* appeared to acclaim. Much of this great work is devoted to Ireland, where he carried out extensive research. His intent was to counteract the hostile portrait of the Irish in J.A. Froude's *The English in Ireland in the Eighteenth Century*, though his own view of contemporary Ireland was that 'the classes who possess political power in Ireland are radically and profoundly unfit for self-government'. The final volume was published in 1890 and was followed in 1892 by a cabinet edition separating the English and Irish histories.

Lecky opposed Home Rule in letters and articles in the major journals. Nonetheless, when in 1895 he was elected MP for Dublin University, his first speech was on behalf of Fenian prisoners. He supported the creation of a Roman Catholic university in Ireland. Later publications were *Democracy and Liberty* (1896), a discursive work on politics, *The Map of Life* (1899), and a revision of *Leaders* (1903), which was finally accepted as a valuable assessment of Flood, Grattan and O'Connell. Ill health forced Lecky to resign from parliament in 1902, the year in which he received the Order of Merit, and he died in London on 22 October 1903.

JOHN PENTLAND MAHAFFY
1839-1919
SCHOLAR

Mahaffy was born near Vevay, in Switzerland, on 26 February

1839. His father was an Irish clergyman, his mother an heiress whose income allowed the young couple to live abroad. They returned to Newbliss, Co. Monaghan, during the potato famine, and had moved to Dublin by the time Mahaffy entered Trinity College in 1855. He was the outstanding scholar of his year, and in 1864 he was elected fellow and ordained. In 1865, he married Frances McDougall, a solicitor's daughter. Mahaffy's considerable academic reputation was to rest largely on Greek studies.

Memorial plaque in Dublin

He acknowledged the assistance of Oscar Wilde in his *Social life in Greece from Homer to Menander* (1874), which dealt so frankly with homosexuality that he was persuaded to amend later editions. He also wrote on Kant and Descartes, and Egyptian studies led to his deciphering papyrus documents discovered by the archaeologist Flinders Petrie. An enemy of provincialism, Mahaffy opposed the revival of the Irish language as 'a return to the dark ages'.

He is best remembered, however, as an all-rounder. He was a talented cricketer, crack shot, versatile musician, and cruelly witty conversationalist whom Oliver St John Gogarty called 'the finest talker in Europe'. Typical epigrams are 'In Ireland the inevitable never happens and the unexpected occurs constantly' and 'An Irish atheist is one who wishes to God he could believe in God'. A social climber, Mahaffy exploited cricket to gain entry to the great houses of Europe.

In 1899, he became a senior fellow, but failed in 1904 to become provost, the crown appointment going to the more diplomatic Anthony Traill, who died in September 1914. On hearing of Traill's illness, Mahaffy had commented 'Nothing trivial, I hope'. In November, Mahaffy refused to let 'a man called Pearse' address a Gaelic society meeting in Trinity; a few days later, he was named provost. Mahaffy had drifted 'quietly and silently' towards Home Rule, and in the 1917 Irish Convention proposed a constitution on Swiss lines. He was knighted in 1918, and died on 30 April 1919.

See
Plaque on his home at 38 North Great George's Street, Dublin.

JAMES BROWN ARMOUR
1841-1928
CLERIC

Armour was born at Lisboy, near Ballymoney, Co. Antrim on 20 January 1841. A Presbyterian farmer's son, he entered Queen's College, Belfast, in 1860. His father wanted him to become a clergyman, but Armour had other ideas and taught for a time before completing his degree at Queen's College, Cork. Armour hoped to practise law, but after his father's death he promised a dying brother that he would study for the ministry. In 1869, he was called to the Second (now Trinity) Presbyterian Church in Ballymoney.

In 1883, Armour married Jennie Hamilton, whose great-grandfather had ministered to the United Irishman William Orr at his execution in 1797. A new church was begun in 1884; some saw its unusual octagonal spire as evidence of popery, and this may have contributed to Armour failing to become professor of church history at Magee College, Londonderry, in 1890.

Armour was an active Liberal; he advocated land reform, and believed Tories were exploiting Unionism for the benefit of Anglican landlords. In the 1892 general election, he supported a Liberal Home Ruler in North Antrim, but there and elsewhere Ulster's Protestants declared for the Union, and Armour faced ostracism and intimidation.

His own congregation remained almost entirely loyal however, respecting his adherence to principle even when they disagreed with him. When he collected over 3,500 Presbyterian signatures commending Gladstone's Home Rule policy, Unionists made every effort to discredit him. Always sympathetic to Catholic aspirations, he supported the founding of the National University (in effect, a successor to Newman's Catholic University) in 1908, despite preferring secular education.

Although warned of a heart condition, Armour remained an active opponent of Unionism, describing the signing of the 1912 Ulster Covenant as 'Protestant Fools' Day'. He laid much of the blame for the 1916 Easter Rising on the Unionists' gun-running and readiness to resist an Act of Parliament by force, and argued strongly against Partition. He died on 25 January 1928.

MICHAEL DAVITT
1846-1906
REVOLUTIONARY

Davitt was born at Straide, Co. Mayo, on 25 March 1846. His father was a Catholic smallholder who had once led an agrarian secret society; evicted after the potato famine, he emigrated with his family to Haslingden, Lancashire. Davitt went to work in a cotton mill in 1857, but had his right arm amputated after a machine accident. Disabled, he took the opportunity to attend a Wesleyan school.

He joined the Fenian movement in 1865, and in 1867 took part in the abortive attack on Chester Castle. In 1868, he became organising secretary of the Fenians in England and Scotland, becoming a commercial traveller in firearms to conceal his revolutionary activities. In 1870, he was sentenced to fifteen years' penal servitude for treason felony, but was released from Dartmoor prison on 'ticket of leave' in 1877.

Davitt joined his family in America, and outlined to Irish Americans such as

Davitt statue, Co. Mayo

John Devoy his plan to link the republican movement with land agitation. He and Devoy launched the 'New Departure' in alliance with Charles Stewart Parnell, who became president of the 1879 Irish National Land League.

A 'land war' ensued, and in 1881 the government conceded the 'three Fs' of fair rent, fixity of tenure and free sale. Davitt later opposed the 'Kilmainham Treaty' negotiated by Parnell, and finally rejected his leadership after Parnell's divorce case. By then, Davitt had served further prison terms.

In 1886, he married Mary Yore of Michigan, and admirers presented her with a home at Ballybrack, Co. Dublin, which became known as 'Land League Cottage'. For much of his life, Davitt earned a precarious living as a journalist, his books include *Leaves from a Prison Diary* (1884). Twice elected to parliament and unseated, he finally reached Westminster as

MP for South Mayo in 1895, but withdrew in 1899 as a protest against the Boer War. He died in Dublin on 31 May 1906.

Visit
Museum at Straide (2¼ miles/3.5 km NE of Bellavary, Co. Mayo), where a plaque and high cross mark Davitt's grave.

CHARLES STEWART PARNELL
1846-1891
POLITICIAN

Parnell was born at Avondale, Co. Wicklow, on 27 June 1846. His father, a wealthy Anglo-Irish landlord, died in 1859; his mother was an American whose father had fought Britain in the War of 1812. Parnell left Cambridge University in 1869 after a drunken brawl, and might have remained a country squire. However, the execution of the 'Manchester martyrs' in 1867 had intensified an instinctive hostility to England, and in 1875 he was elected Home Rule MP for Co. Meath.

Parnell statue, Dublin

Parnell's obstructive tactics proved so successful that he became president of the Irish National Land League in 1879, and leader of the parliamentary party in 1880. In 1876, he shocked the Commons by denying that the killing of a constable during the 1867 rescue of Fenians in Manchester was 'murder'. Parnell's loose understanding with Michael Davitt and the American Fenian John Devoy was known as the 'New Departure'. He believed that, once land reform was achieved, Protestant landlords would have no reason to support the Union. In October 1881, Parnell was arrested and held in Kilmainham Jail, Dublin, with other Land League leaders. When they called on their followers not to pay rents, the League was declared illegal, but the government was forced into the reforms of the 'Kilmainham Treaty', and Parnell was released in May 1882.

After the 1885 election, 'The Chief' and his eighty-five MPs held the balance of power at Westminster, but Gladstone's Home Rule measure was defeated in 1886. In 1887, articles on 'Parnell and Crime' in *The Times* were shown to be based on forgeries. In 1889, Parnell was cited as co-respondent in a divorce case brought by an Irish MP whose wife, Katherine O'Shea, had been Parnell's mistress since 1880. Parnell later married his 'Queenie', but his popular support had waned, and he lost the leadership of a divided party. Worn out by three by-elections in which Parnellite candidates were defeated, he died in Brighton on 6 October 1891.

Visit

Avondale (1½ miles/2 km S of Rathdrum, Co. Wicklow).

See

Statue by Augustus St Gaudens in O'Connell Street Dublin.

WILLIAM JAMES PIRRIE,
VISCOUNT PIRRIE
1847-1924
SHIPBUILDER

Pirrie was born of Ulster parents in Quebec, Canada, on 31 May 1847. He spent his childhood at Conlig, Co. Down, and at fifteen was apprenticed to the Harland & Wolff shipyard in Belfast. He worked his way through different departments, and in 1874 was taken into partnership by the two founders of the firm, Sir Edward Harland and G.W. Wolff. Pirrie succeeded Harland as the shipyard's driving force, and was for many years its chairman.

Harland & Wolff Shipyard

Modern steel-making revolutionised shipbuilding, and Pirrie was at the forefront of development in marine engineering and naval architecture, particularly in building large ships such as the 46,000-ton *Olympic* (1911) and the 48,000-ton *Britannic* (1914). Harland had formed a connection with the new White Star Line in 1869, and Pirrie's 'floating hotels' maintained their supremacy in the North Atlantic. His own extensive travels helped him to understand passengers' needs; only illness prevented him joining the *Titanic* on her ill-fated maiden voyage in 1912.

Both founders of the shipyard had become MPs. Pirrie chose instead to serve on Belfast Corporation, becoming Lord Mayor in 1896-97. He was active in extending the city's boundary, beginning a new City Hall, and launching a scheme to build what became the Royal Victoria Hospital. His Unionist views had so weakened that he was refused nomination as a Unionist parliamentary candidate in 1902; backing Liberal candidates in the 1906 election, he soon became Baron Pirrie.

Pirrie's support for the 1912 Home Rule Bill made him unpopular in Belfast, and he was jeered in the streets after chairing a famous meeting of the Ulster Liberal Association addressed by Winston Churchill. During World War I, he turned his yards over to warship construction, and inaugurated a large aircraft department. In 1918, he became comptroller-general of merchant shipbuilding, and was energetic in replacing tonnage lost through submarine warfare. He received his viscountcy in 1921, when King George V opened the new Northern Ireland parliament, but had no heir. He died at sea on 7 June 1924.

SARAH PURSER
1848-1943
ARTIST

Sarah Purser was born in Kingstown (now Dun Laoghaire) Co. Dublin, on 22 March 1848. Her father emigrated to America when his flour-milling business failed, and she lived with her mother, studying at the Dublin School of Art and then in Paris.

After exhibiting at the Royal Hibernian Academy, she was invited to paint the future Countess Markievicz and her sister Eva Gore-Booth. This led to other commissions and, in her own words, she 'went through the British aristocracy like measles'. In 1901 she organised a notable exhibition of the paintings of Nathaniel Hone and John B. Yeats. A visitor was Hugh Lane, and she painted Douglas Hyde and others for Lane's projected collection of national portraits.

Another friend was Edward Martyn, who was advising on a new Roman Catholic cathedral in Loughrea, Co. Galway, and wanted to involve Irish artists. The outcome was *An Túr Gloine* (The Tower of Glass), a workshop for stained glass which Sarah established in 1903 at 24 Upper Pembroke Street, Dublin. Its most notable artists were to be Michael Healy and Evie Hone.

In 1911, Sarah and her brother John, a professor of medicine, moved into Mespil House (since destroyed), an eighteenth-century mansion beside the Grand Canal. Her monthly salon, 'Miss Purser's second Tuesdays', became a Dublin institution and an opportunity to exercise her waspish tongue. A typical comment – on an Irish memoirist – was 'Some men kiss and tell, but George Moore tells and doesn't kiss'.

With the establishment of the Irish Free State, Sarah became friendly with W.T. Cosgrave, and in 1928 persuaded him that Charlemont House in Parnell Square, recently vacated by a government department should become the Municipal Gallery of Modern Art which Lane had sought. She still painted in her eighties and was almost ninety when she made Oliver St John Gogarty fly her over Mespil House to inspect the roof. She died in Dublin on 7 August 1943.

See

Stained glass in St Brendan's Cathedral, Loughrea.

LADY GREGORY
1852-1932
PLAYWRIGHT

Augusta Persse was born on 15 March 1852 at Roxborough House, near Loughrea, Co. Galway. In 1880, she married Sir William Gregory, of nearby Coole Park, a retired governor of Ceylon; he was thirty-five years older, and died in 1892. His widow edited his *Autobiography* (1894), and compiled *Mr Gregory's Letter Box* (1898), dealing with his grandfather's correspondence as Irish under-secretary.

A childhood nurse had introduced her to Irish folklore and fairy tales. Her background reading now converted her to Home Rule, and she later wrote 'I defy anyone to study Irish history without getting a dislike and distrust of England.' She met W.B. Yeats in London and at the home of her neighbour, Edward Martyn, and together they planned a national theatre.

The first production of the Irish Literary Theatre in Dublin was Yeats' *The Countess Cathleen* (1899). In 1904, the Abbey Theatre opened with her comedy *Spreading the News* and Yeats' *On Baile's Strand*. Lady Gregory wrote over thirty plays, including comedies such as *The Workhouse Ward* (1908) and 'folk history' plays such as *Kincora* (1905),which drew modern lessons from the story of Brian Boru.

Lady Gregory also met Douglas Hyde, and formed a branch of his Gaelic League at Kiltartan, the village at Coole; she wrote often in 'Kiltartan', a stage dialect using grammatical constructions from the Irish language. She collected folklore enthusiastically, and published *Cuchulain of Muirthemne* and *Gods and Fighting Men* (1904).

Coole Park was the headquarters of the Irish Literary Revival, attracting many visitors. An aunt of Hugh Lane, Lady Gregory campaigned vigorously after his death for the Lane pictures to be returned from London to Dublin. Roxburgh was burned down in the Civil War; Coole was sold to the Irish Land Commission in 1927, but Lady Gregory was able to occupy the house and garden until her death on 22 May 1932.

Visit

Coole Park (2 miles/3 km N of Gort, Co. Galway), with 'autograph tree' bearing initials of famous visitors. The former national school at Kiltartan is now a Gregory museum.

EDWARD CARSON,
LORD CARSON
1854-1935
BARRISTER AND POLITICIAN

Carson was born at 4 Harcourt Street, Dublin, on 9 February 1854. Educated at Trinity College, Dublin, he was called to the Irish Bar in 1877, taking silk in 1889. As counsel to the Irish attorney-general, he became known as 'Coercion Carson'.

Carson statue, Stormont

In 1892, Carson was appointed solicitor-general for Ireland, but on being elected Liberal Unionist MP for his university he found himself in opposition. He made his maiden speech at Westminster from the front bench and was a vigorous critic of Gladstone's Home Rule Bill in 1893. In 1894, he became the first Irish QC to take silk in England, and his cross-examination of Oscar Wilde in 1895 demonstrated his courtroom skills. In 1910, in a case later dramatised in Terence Rattigan's *The Winslow Boy* (1946), he established the innocence of a naval cadet accused of stealing a postal order.

In 1910, now knighted, Carson agreed to lead the Irish Unionist parliamentary party. His loyal lieutenant was Capt. James Craig, at whose house overlooking Belfast Lough he addressed a large rally in 1911, describing the imminent Home Rule Bill as 'the most nefarious conspiracy that has ever been hatched against a free people'. On 'Ulster Day', 28 September 1912, a covenant to defeat Home Rule attracted 471,414 signatures. The Ulster Volunteer Force was formed in 1913 and, on the outbreak of World War I, Carson committed its men to the British Army. The Home Rule legislation was suspended.

In 1918, recognising that Home Rule could not be prevented outside Ulster, he became MP for the Belfast constituency of Duncairn at Westminster, and in 1921 Craig became Unionist leader and prime minister in the new Northern Ireland parliament. Carson became a lord of appeal in 1921, with a life peerage as Baron Carson of Duncairn. A disillusioned man, he concluded that 'I was only a puppet, and so was Ulster, and so was Ireland, in the political game to get the Conservative Party into power.' He quit the bench in 1929, and died in Kent on 22 October 1935.

See

Statue by L.S. Merrifield at Stormont, Belfast.

SIR HORACE PLUNKETT
1854-1932
PIONEER OF CO-OPERATION

Plunkett was born at Sherborne House, Gloucestershire on 24 October 1854. He was the third son of the 16th Baron Dunsany, whose seat was in Co. Meath, his mother was a daughter of the 2nd Baron Sherborne. In 1879, lung trouble persuaded Plunkett to seek a better climate as a rancher in Wyoming. Ten years later, he returned to Ireland, but visited America annually.

In 1889, Plunkett established the first co-operative creamery in Ireland, at Drumcolliher, Co. Limerick. The movement soon spread, and in 1894 he became first

President of the new Irish Agricultural Organisation Society, holding office until 1899. In 1891, he had become a member of the Congested Districts Board, and in 1892 was elected Unionist MP for South Co. Dublin. The report of a committee convened on his initiative led to the establishment in 1899 of the Department of Agricultural and Technical Instruction. Plunkett became its political head, and held office until 1907. He was knighted in 1903.

Plunkett's slogan, adopted in America by Theodore Roosevelt, was 'Better farming, better business, better living'. He saw state aid as an encouragement to self-help, not a substitute for it. In 1907, he was again elected President of the IAOS, and a year later public subscription purchased a headquarters at 84 Merrion Square, Dublin, known as Plunkett House. His visionary ideas were largely frustrated by commercial and political interests, however, and ultimately Plunkett enjoyed greater esteem outside Ireland.

While striving to keep his movement non-political Plunkett himself was converted to Home Rule and in 1914 published an 'Appeal to Ulster not to desert Ireland'. In 1917-18, he chaired the unsuccessful Irish Convention and in 1919 founded the Irish Dominion League in the hope of keeping Ireland within the British Commonwealth. He became a senator in the new Irish Free State and republicans responded in 1923 by burning down his house, Kilteragh, at Foxrock, Co. Dublin. He then settled at Weybridge, in Surrey, where he died on 26 March 1932.

SIR JOHN LAVERY
1856-1941
ARTIST

Lavery was born in Belfast in 1856. His father was drowned in 1859 on his way to America, his mother died of grief, and three orphans were divided among relatives. Lavery went first to an uncle's farm near Moira, Co. Down, then to another relative in Saltcoats, Ayrshire. He was apprenticed a Glasgow artist and photographer, and studied at the Glasgow School of Art.

At twenty, he set up as an independent artist in Glasgow, enduring poverty until a studio fire brought £300 insurance money, which he used to study in London and Paris. In 1886, the Royal Academy accepted his painting of *A Tennis Party*. He became one of the 'Glasgow School' painters, and was commissioned to paint Queen Victoria's state visit in 1888; when the Queen agreed to sit for him, success as a portraitist was assured. In 1890, he married his model, Kathleen MacDermott, but she died after giving birth to a daughter.

After many rejections by the Royal Academy, Lavery and James McNeill Whistler formed the rival International Society of Sculptors, Painters and Gravers in 1897. In 1910, he married Hazel Trudeau, a widowed American artist little older than his daughter. After acting as a war artist, he was knighted in 1918; he became a British Academician in 1921.

Lavery was generally more successful in portraying women, but an interest in the Irish question led him to paint Griffith, Carson, de Valera, Cosgrave and Collins, as well as the 1916 trial of Casement. During the negotiations on the Anglo-Irish Treaty of 1921, Lavery and his wife entertained lavishly in London; in *The Life of a Painter* (1940) Lavery affirmed 'By many it was believed that had it not been for Hazel there would have been no Treaty – certainly not at the time.'

Lady Lavery had hopes of occupying the vice-regal lodge in Dublin, but had to be content with having her portrait on the new Irish banknotes, her husband painting her as the symbolic Cathleen ni Houlihan. Lavery continued to paint into his eighties – in 1936, he portrayed his encounter with Shirley Temple in Hollywood – and died in Kilkenny on 10 January 1941.

See
A blue plaque marks the site of Lavery's birthplace, 47 North Queen Street.

DOUGLAS HYDE
1860-1949
GAELIC SCHOLAR

Hyde was born at Castlerea, Co. Roscommon, on 17 January 1860. Six years later his father became rector at Frenchpark, Co. Roscommon. Douglas Hyde spent his formative years there, acquiring a knowledge of Irish from native speakers. He had a distinguished career at Trinity College, Dublin becoming a doctor of laws in 1888 after he had decided not to take holy orders.

Frenchpark, Co. Roscommon

As a young man, Hyde had published poems in Irish, using the pen-name An Craoibhín Aoibhinn (the delightful little branch) by which he was later widely known. On returning from a brief period of teaching in Canada, he settled at Ratra House, Frenchpark, and thereafter devoted himself to preserving the language. He had published a collection of folk tales in Irish in 1889, and many were translated into English in *Beside the fire* (1890). However, it was *Love Songs of Connacht* (1893), in which his translations accompanied Irish originals, which attracted most attention. This was followed by *Poems ascribed to Raftery* (1903) and *The Religious Songs of Connacht* (1906).

In 1892, Hyde became president of the National Literary Society. Following a presidential address calling for the Irish nation to be 'de-Anglicised', he was invited to chair the 1893 meeting from which the Gaelic League emerged. Hyde was immensely active and successful as its first president, but ultimately he was unable to prevent the League becoming a political battleground. When in 1915 the organisation committed itself to the objective of a 'free, Gaelic-speaking Ireland', Hyde resigned both his presidency and his membership. He had become professor of modern Irish at University College, Dublin, in 1909 and held this post until 1932. He also wrote plays for the Abbey Theatre. Hyde was briefly a senator of the Irish Free State in 1925-6 and again in 1937, but it was as a widely respected figure above politics that in 1938 he was chosen as first president of Ireland under a new constitution. He held office until his term expired in 1945, and died in Dublin on 12 July 1949.

ROGER CASEMENT
1864-1916
REVOLUTIONARY

Casement was born in Sandycove, Co. Dublin, on 1 September 1864. His Protestant father, an army officer who in 1848 had helped Hungarian rebels against Austrian rule, and Catholic mother both died before he was ten, and he was raised by an uncle in Ballycastle, Co. Antrim. At twenty, he sailed as a purser to West Africa, and joined the explorer Henry Stanley's Congo International Association, whose aims included suppression of slavery and improvement of natives' conditions. In 1892, he entered government service, holding consular posts in Africa.

Casement's investigation of the rubber industry in the Congo disclosed a system of slave labour enforced by flogging and mutilation, and his 1904 report led to the eventual abolition of the Congo Free State. He was knighted in 1911, having also exposed ill-treatment of Peruvian Indians in rubber plantations, and retired to Ireland in 1913.

Casement had come to think of Ireland as an enslaved and exploited country, and he became active in the Irish Volunteers. When war broke out in 1914, the Nationalist leader John Redmond encouraged Volunteers to join the British Army. Casement, in contrast sought aid from Germany, which he admired as a colonial power. The Germans agreed to send arms in the trawler *Aud* for the planned 1916 rising, and Casement followed by submarine. Three days before the rising, the *Aud* was captured off the Kerry coast; Casement, who had landed at Tralee Bay, was arrested and charged with treason.

He was sentenced to death in London, and a campaign for a reprieve lost momentum when copies of the so-called 'Black Diaries' were circulated to demonstrate to influential opinion that Casement had been an active homosexual; controversy has since raged over their authenticity. Stripped of his honours, Casement was hanged on 3 August 1916, having first been received into the Catholic Church. In 1965, his remains were reinterred in Glasnevin Cemetery, Dublin.

See
Memorial marking Casement's landing at Banna Strand, Co. Kerry.
Casement monument at Murlough Bay, Co. Antrim.

MAUD GONNE MacBRIDE
1865-1953
REVOLUTIONARY

Maud Gonne was born near Aldershot, in England, probably on 20 December 1865. Her mother died in 1871 and, when her army officer father was posted to Dublin Castle in 1882, she acted as his hostess. Col. Gonne died in 1886, and Maud and her sister lived briefly with an uncle in London. Contracting a lung haemorrhage, she was sent to recover to the French Auvergne, where she met Lucien Millevoye, a journalist and politician whose marriage had broken down. She was to bear him two children before their affair ended in 1898.

Dublin Castle

The couple agreed to work together for Irish independence and for French recovery of Alsace-Lorraine from Germany. Millevoye suggested that Maud, though English, could become Ireland's Joan of Arc. With W.B. Yeats, she founded an Association Irlandaise in Paris, but rejected his marriage proposals. She joined the secret Irish Republican Brotherhood, and attracted police attention in Ireland by her protests against eviction and against celebration of Queen Victoria's diamond jubilee.

In 1900, she founded *Inghinidhe na hÉireann* (Daughters of Ireland), a women's republican movement, and opposed Boer War recruitment. In 1902, she played Yeats' *Cathleen ni Houlihan*, symbolising Ireland's struggle when she shed the appearance of an old crone to become 'a young girl with the walk of a queen'. In 1903, she married in Paris Maj. John MacBride, who had formed an Irish brigade to fight on the Boers' side; their marriage failed, and he returned to Ireland, where he was executed after the 1916 rising. She spent most of her time in France.

Returning to Dublin, she was interned in 1918 and spent some months in Holloway prison in London. She organised relief during the War of Independence, and assisted republican prisoners and their dependants during the Civil War. Imprisoned in 1923, she was released after going on hunger strike. In 1938, she published an account of her early life, *A Servant of the Queen*. From 1922, she lived at Roebuck House, Clonskeagh, Dublin, where she died on 27 April 1953.

EOIN MacNEILL
1867-1945
GAELIC SCHOLAR

John MacNeill, as he was baptised, was born in Glenarm, Co. Antrim, on 15 May 1867. In 1887, he won a clerkship in the Four Courts in Dublin, where he developed an interest in Irish. In 1893, an article by MacNeill on preserving Irish led to the foundation of the Gaelic League. He became honorary secretary, and Douglas Hyde president. Over four hundred branches were formed within ten years.

MacNeill was appointed editor of the monthly *Gaelic Journal* in 1894, and of the new weekly *An Claidheam Soluis* in 1899, then vice-president of the League in 1903. In 1909, he became professor of early Irish history at University College, Dublin, where he successfully argued that Irish should be a compulsory matriculation subject. From writings such as *Phases of Irish History* (1919) and *Celtic Ireland* (1921) it is evident that MacNeill saw the language as essential to Irish nationality.

In November 1913, he contributed an influential leading article, 'The North Began', to the weekly, calling for the formation of Irish Volunteers in response to the Unionists' Ulster Volunteers. He became president and later chief of staff, believing the Volunteers would ensure Home Rule. However, when in 1916 he discovered that Patrick Pearse and others planned to turn Volunteer manoeuvres into an armed uprising, he cancelled orders for Easter Sunday parades. The abortive rising went ahead, and a court-martial sentenced MacNeill to penal servitude for life. While in prison in England, he was elected president of the Gaelic League.

Released under an amnesty in 1917, MacNeill was elected Sinn Féin MP for both Londonderry and the National University, and later became minister of education in the Irish Free State. In 1923, he was also appointed to the Boundary Commission set up to determine the border between the two parts of a partitioned Ireland, but resigned in 1925 during the uproar caused by a well informed newspaper forecast that only minor changes in the existing border would be recommended. MacNeill returned to scholarship, becoming first chairman of the Irish Manuscripts Commission in 1928. He died in Dublin on 15 October 1945.

CONSTANCE MARKIEVICZ
1868-1927
REVOLUTIONARY

Constance Gore-Booth was born in London on 4 February 1868. Her father soon inherited estates at Lissadell, Co. Sligo, where W.B. Yeats later recalled Constance and her sister Eva as 'Two girls in silk kimonos, both Beautiful, one a gazelle'. She had an adventurous nature and was a noted horsewoman.

In 1898, studying art in Paris, she met Count Casimir Dunin-Markievicz. He was Polish, six years younger, a painter and Roman Catholic, with an estranged wife dying in the Ukraine. The couple married in 1900, and settled in 1903, later renting a cottage in the Dublin mountains.

Lissadell House, Co. Sligo

The poet Padraic Colum had left old copies of *Sinn Féin* there and, reading them, Constance was converted to the cause of Irish independence. Taking part in a Sinn Féin demonstration, she effectively severed her links with Dublin Castle. In 1909, she founded Na Fianna Éireann, a republican movement for boys, who received arms training at the cottage. She organised a soup kitchen during the 1913 strike in Dublin. Her neglected husband left Ireland, and did not return to Dublin until 1924.

Countess Markievicz joined the Irish Citizen Army under James Connolly and in the 1916 rising occupied the College of Surgeons at St Stephen's Green. Her death sentence was commuted; while in prison, she was elected president of Cumann na mBan, the women's auxiliary force of the Irish Volunteers.

Released in 1917, she was received into the Catholic Church. Arrested again in 1918, she was in prison when elected Sinn Féin MP for a Dublin constituency; the first woman elected to Westminster, on release she sat instead in the separatist Dáil Éireann, becoming minister for labour.

Rejecting the 1921 Anglo-Irish Treaty, she toured America in the republican cause. Countess Markievicz eventually joined the Fianna Fáil party formed by Eamon de Valera (*see page 103*), and was elected to the Dáil shortly before her death in Dublin on 15 July 1927.

Visit
Lissadell House (8 miles/13 km N of Sligo).

See
Bust by Seamus Murphy in St Stephen's Green, Dublin.

JAMES CONNOLLY
1868-1916
REVOLUTIONARY SOCIALIST

Connolly was born in Cowgate, Edinburgh, on 5 June 1868. His Irish Catholic parents were poor, and Connolly worked from the age of eleven; in 1882, he falsified his age to join the army. Stationed in Dublin in 1889, he deserted to avoid foreign service. In 1890, he married Lillie Reynolds, a Protestant domestic servant from Co. Wicklow, and returned to Edinburgh.

Politically active in Scotland, Connolly became paid organiser of the Dublin Socialist Club in 1906. He founded and became secretary of the Irish Socialist Republican Party, and in 1898 launched the weekly *Workers' Republic*, exploiting the 1798 centenary to argue that only in a socialist republic could the ideals of Wolfe Tone be realised. He later worked for the new Socialist Labour Party in Scotland, and helped to found the International Workers of the World (the 'Wobblies') in America.

Connolly returned to Ireland in 1910, joining the Socialist Party of Ireland, successor to the ISRP. He soon published

Labour, Nationality and Religion, defending a Catholic's right to be a socialist, and *Labour in Irish History*, describing the working class as 'the incorruptible inheritors of the fight for freedom in Ireland'. In 1911, he became Ulster organiser of the Irish Transport and General Workers' Union, headed by James Larkin, and soon called a dock strike in Belfast. When Larkin was imprisoned in 1913, Connolly forced his release by closing the port of Dublin.

Larkin left for America in 1914, and Connolly became acting secretary of the ITGWU, commandant of the recently formed Irish Citizen Army, and editor of the *Irish Worker*, which was soon suppressed for its anti-war sentiments. He was persuaded by the Irish Republican Brotherhood to support the 1916 rising, and about 120 ICA members took part. Connolly was commandant-general in Dublin, and led the assault on the General Post Office. His left ankle was smashed by a bullet, and after his court martial he was shot at Kilmainham Jail on 12 May 1916.

Visit
Kilmainham Jail Museum, Dublin.

ERSKINE CHILDERS
1870-1922
AUTHOR AND REVOLUTIONARY

Childers was born in London on 25 June 1870. His English father died in 1876, his Anglo-Irish mother in 1884. Much of his childhood was spent at his mother's home, Glendalough House, Annamoe, Co. Wicklow. At nineteen, sciatica gave him a permanent limp.

Childers was educated in England, and in 1895 became a committee clerk in the House of Commons. Serving in the Boer War, he published his war diary and wrote two war histories, campaigning against the use of antiquated cavalry. However, his reputation as a writer rests on *The Riddle of the Sands* (1903); his story of two yachtsmen chancing on a German plan to invade England impressed readers fearful of German militarism.

In 1903, he married Mollie Osgood, daughter of a Boston doctor, her father's wedding present was a yacht, the *Asgard*. The Boer War had made Childers question Britain's imperial role, and in time he espoused the Home Rule cause. He resigned from the Commons in 1910, and urged dominion status for Ireland in *The Framework of Home Rule* (1911). After the Ulster gun-running of April 1914, Childers used the *Asgard* to land arms for the Irish Volunteers at Howth, Co. Dublin, on 26 July 1914.

Childers served in the Royal Navy and Royal Air Force in World War I, and in 1917 was seconded to the secretariat of the Irish Convention. In 1919, he accompanied Arthur Griffith to the Versailles peace conference. Settling in Dublin, he was elected to Dáil Éireann, and became secretary to the Irish delegation which negotiated the 1921 Anglo-Irish Treaty.

By now a fanatical republican, Childers opposed the treaty, Griffith responding 'I will not reply to any damned Englishman in this assembly'. During the Civil War, the former British officer became increasingly isolated among the guerrillas of Co. Cork. He was captured at Glendalough House, and after a court-martial was executed in Dublin on 24 November 1922. In 1973, his son and namesake became the fourth president of Ireland.

Visit

Kilmainham Jail Museum, Dublin, with the *Asgard* and other gun-running exhibits.

JAMES CRAIG,
VISCOUNT CRAIGAVON
1871-1940
POLITICIAN

Craig was born at Sydenham, Belfast, on 8 January 1871. His father was a Presbyterian whiskey distiller, a self-made millionaire who soon bought a substantial house, Craigavon, overlooking Belfast Lough. Craig became a successful stockbroker, then saw service in the Boer War. Captured in 1900, he chose to march 200 miles with his men rather than ride with his fellow officers; released because of a war wound, he was eventually invalided home with dysentery.

A legacy enabled him to turn to politics, and he represented Co. Down constituencies as a Unionist from 1906 to 1921. In 1911, when a new Home Rule Bill was imminent, Craig staged a massive unionist rally at Craigavon, at which Sir Edward Carson assumed leadership of northern Protestants. Craig's organisational skills and courage allied to Carson's oratory built Ulster unionism into a powerful force.

With the outbreak of war in 1914, Home Rule was put into abeyance. Craig immediately offered the Ulster Volunteer Force, which had been drilling since 1912, to the British Army. It became the 36th (Ulster) Division, suffering heavily at the Somme in 1916. Ill health denied Craig active service.

In 1920, a new parliament was established for six of the nine Ulster counties. With Carson opting to remain at Westminster, Craig became Northern Ireland's first prime minister. In violent times, he established a new police force, the Royal Ulster Constabulary, supported by a special constabulary and equipped with exceptional powers. However, while restoring order, he also tried to reach some understanding with southern leaders such as Eamon de Valera and Michael Collins, and was more tolerant of the Catholic minority in Northern Ireland than most of his followers.

Craig ensured that the boundary commission set up under the 1921 treaty did not reduce Northern Ireland's territory, but he and his ageing cabinet made little progress on social and economic problems. He became Viscount Craigavon of Stormont in 1927, and died at Glencraig, Co. Down, on 24 November 1940.

ARTHUR GRIFFITH
1871-1922
POLITICIAN

Griffith was born at 4 Dominick Street, Dublin, on 31 March 1871. He was apprenticed as a compositor, and in 1897 sailed to South Africa, partly for health reasons. He edited an English weekly newspaper, then worked in gold mining; in Johannesburg, he organised a parade to celebrate the centenary of the 1798 rising.

Returning to Dublin, he and William Rooney founded a weekly newspaper, *The United Irishman*, named after one associated with John Mitchel in 1848. Griffith wanted Irish MPs to stay away from Westminster. His articles were republished as *The Resurrection of Hungary, A Parallel for Ireland* (1904), arguing that Hungarians had won independence from Austria in 1867 by refusing to send representatives to the parliament in Vienna.

In 1903, Griffith formed the National Council, and in 1905 elaborated his ideas under the name Sinn Féin (Ourselves Alone). When *The United Irishman* was bankrupted by a libel action in 1906, he launched a new publication, *Sinn Féin*. A Sinn Féin party gradually emerged, and Griffith became president in 1911; he joined the Irish Volunteers in 1913. An opponent of insurrection, Griffith took no part in the 1916 rising, but was interned in England for some months. It was widely but wrongly described as a Sinn Féin rising, and his party gained impetus.

He yielded the presidency to Eamon de Valera in 1917, and the party's successes in the 1918 election paved the way to the War of Independence. Dáil Éireann, the alternative assembly Griffith had envisaged, met in January 1919, and he became home affairs minister and deputy president. Griffith led the delegation which negotiated the 1921 Anglo-Irish Treaty. After the Dáil rejected de Valera's opposition to its terms, Griffith was elected president of the Dáil and of the 'Republic of Ireland' which was soon to be replaced by the Irish Free State. The treaty was endorsed in the general election of June 1922, but the Civil War quickly followed. An exhausted Griffith died suddenly in Dublin on 12 August 1922.

See

Memorial at Leinster Lawn, Merrion Square, Dublin.

JACK B. YEATS
1871-1957
ARTIST

Jack Butler Yeats was the youngest of the five children of the painter John B. Yeats. His father had barely finished art school when Yeats was born in London on 29 August 1871. Yeats spent much of his childhood with his mother's parents in Sligo, where he sketched with equal enthusiasm the town's quays and the surrounding countryside. Returning to London in 1887, he studied art and began to illustrate magazines. Boxing and horse-racing were favourite subjects, often tackled humorously.

In 1894, he married Mary Cottenham White, a Devon artist. In 1895, his water-colour of *Strand races, West of Ireland* was accepted by the Royal Hibernian Academy. Since photography now threatened traditional illustrations, he developed this side of his talent, exhibiting in London and Dublin. Lady Gregory saw his work as complementing the Irish Literary Revival in which his brother W.B. Yeats was deeply involved. He illustrated articles by J.M. Synge and also his book on *The Aran Islands*. Other drawings accompanied broadsheet poems produced by the Cuala Press, and in 1912 he published *Life in the West of Ireland*.

Yeats and 'Cottie' moved from Devon to Ireland in 1910, and he worked increasingly in oils. Paintings such as *Bachelor's Walk: In Memory* (1915) and *The Funeral of Harry Boland* (1922) reflected the unsettled times. Later, his careful draughtsmanship gave way to broader brush work and richer colours, with mystical titles such as *A Race in Hy-Brazil* (1937) and *And Graine saw this sun sink* (1950).

Many Yeats paintings have a narrative element, and not surprisingly he turned to writing. His novels included *Sailing, Sailing Swiftly* (1933) and *The Aramanthers* (1936), and plays such as *La La Noo* (1942) and *In Sand* (1949) were staged at the Abbey Theatre. However, none of his writing has the impact of the evocatively Irish drawings and paintings which, late in his life, established an international reputation. He died in Dublin on 28 March 1957.

Visit

The Yeats Museum in the National Gallery, Dublin, a permanent collection of works by Yeats and his father.

See

A plaque marks Yeats' home at 18 Fitzwilliam Square, Dublin.

SIR HUGH LANE
1875-1915
ART COLLECTOR

Hugh Lane was born on 9 November 1875 at Ballybrack, Co. Cork, where his father was rector. His mother, Adelaide Persse, was a sister of Lady Gregory (*see page 77*), and she travelled extensively in Europe with her son. Lane was apprenticed to the London art dealer Martin Colnaghi, and in 1898 opened his own gallery. His flair for judging paintings quickly made him rich.

Hugh Lane Gallery

In 1900, he visited his aunt at Coole Park, Co. Galway, and met W.B. Yeats and others involved in the Irish Literary Revival. Lane proposed a Dublin gallery to house modern works of art, and commissioned John B. Yeats to paint leading Irish figures. In 1904, he staged a Dublin exhibition of French paintings, many of which were bought for the proposed gallery.

Dublin Corporation provided a temporary gallery in Harcourt Street, which at its 1908 opening had paintings by Corot, Daumier, Degas, Millet and Constable. Lavery (*see page 81*) presented several paintings. Lane also lent thirty-nine paintings, mostly by French impressionists, promising to donate them when there was a permanent gallery. He was knighted in 1909.

At Lane's request, Sir Edward Lutyens designed a gallery, proposing an imaginative building to span the river Liffey. When Dublin Corporation rejected the scheme in 1913, Lane angrily removed his paintings and bequeathed them to the National Gallery in London, which meanwhile had them on loan. In 1914, he was appointed director of the National Gallery in Dublin. In 1915, about to visit America, he added an unwitnessed codicil to his will leaving the paintings to Dublin provided that a suitable building was found within five years of his death. He was drowned on 7 May 1915, when the *Lusitania* was torpedoed.

The Lane pictures provoked years of controversy and, although a permanent gallery was established in Parnell Square in 1933, the British and Irish governments only reached agreement in 1959 to divide the collection into two groups, each being loaned to Dublin for five-year periods. A revised agreement, more generous to Dublin, was concluded in 1979.

Visit
The Hugh Lane Gallery, Parnell Square, Dublin.

JAMES LARKIN
1876-1947
TRADE UNIONIST

Larkin was born in Liverpool on 21 January 1876. The son of poor Irish emigrants, he worked from the age of nine, becoming a foreman docker before losing his job for siding with strikers. He then became an organiser for the National Union of Dock Labourers, commanding allegiance with mesmeric oratory.

In 1907, Larkin fought a lockout in Belfast docks, using new methods of 'blacking' goods and encouraging sympathy strikes, but his English-based union took fright at his militancy. He moved to Dublin, where in 1909 he formed the Irish Transport and General Workers' Union. As general secretary, he recruited thousands of members among the city's unskilled slum dwellers. He spent three months in prison in 1910, on a charge of misusing union money, but his popularity was undimmed.

Larkin statue, Dublin

In 1913, principal Dublin employers determined to destroy Larkin's union. They were led by William Martin Murphy, proprietor of the *Irish Independent* and director of the Dublin United Tramways Company, who demanded pledges of loyalty from employees. The ITGWU 'blacked' Murphy's newspapers and abandoned trams; soon, thousands of workers were locked out.

'Big Jim' was charged with seditious conspiracy, but evaded arrest until he appeared in disguise at a proscribed meeting; a scuffle led to police baton charges, and two people were killed. He was sentenced to seven months' imprisonment, but was soon released when James Connolly closed Dublin port. The strikers admitted defeat in 1914, but the ITGWU survived; the lockout led to the formation of the Irish Citizen Army.

Larkin set out for America in 1914, hoping to raise funds; he returned in 1923, having served almost three years in Sing Sing prison for 'criminal anarchy'. After a legal action which bankrupted him, Larkin was expelled from the ITGWU in

1924. With his brother Peter, he founded the Workers' Union of Ireland, gravely weakening Labour as a political force. He was active in international Communism, and also sat for brief periods in the Dáil. Larkin died in Dublin on 30 January 1947.

See
Statue by Oisin Kelly in O'Connell Street, Dublin.

PATRICK PEARSE
1879-1916
REVOLUTIONARY

Patrick Henry Pearse (Pádraic or Pádraig Mac Piarais) was born on 10 November 1879 at 27 Great Brunswick (now Pearse) Street, Dublin. His father was an English stonemason, his mother came from Co. Meath. Pearse developed a love of the Irish language at the Christian Brothers school in Westland Row, and joined the Gaelic League in 1896, soon going on to its executive.

Pearse's Cottage

He graduated from the Royal University in 1901, and was called to the Bar, but seldom practised. Instead, he helped his younger brother Willie run the family business and taught Irish at University College, Dublin. In 1903, Pearse became editor of the Gaelic League's journal,

An Claidheamh Soluis.

In 1908, Pearse opened a bilingual school for boys, St Enda's, in the Dublin suburb of Rathmines. In 1910, he moved to larger premises at The Hermitage, Rathfarnham, where Robert Emmet had courted Sarah Curran; his first school became St Ita's, for girls, but financial problems forced its closure.

Pearse delivered a notable oration at the Emmet commemoration in 1911, and envisaged dying in an Irish revolution. With Eoin MacNeill and others, he formed the Irish Volunteers in November 1913; a month later, he joined the Irish Republican Brotherhood. In a famous oration in 1915, at the burial of the Fenian O'Donovan Rossa, he ended 'the fools, the fools, the fools they have left us our Fenian dead, and while Ireland holds these graves, Ireland unfree shall never be at peace'.

When the Easter Rising began on 24 April 1916, Pearse read the proclamation of the Irish Republic outside the General Post Office in Sackville (now O'Connell) Street Dublin. He became president of the provisional government and commander-in-chief of the republican army. Five days later, Pearse agreed to an unconditional surrender. On 3 May 1916, following a court-martial, he was executed by a firing squad in Kilmainham Jail. Willie Pearse was one of fourteen others shot dead.

Visit

St Enda's, Grange Road, Farnham, now a Pearse museum; Kilmainham Jail Museum, Dublin; Pearse's summer cottage, near Rosmuc (8½ miles/13.5 km S of Maam Cross, Co. Galway).

WILLIAM T. COSGRAVE
1880-1965
POLITICIAN

Cosgrave was born at 174 James's Street, Dublin, on 6 June 1880. His father, a publican, was a city councillor and Poor Law guardian, so he grew up in a political environment. In 1905, Cosgrave attended the first Sinn Féin convention; he was elected to Dublin Corporation in 1909. He joined the Irish Volunteers in 1913, and in 1916 served under Eamonn Ceannt in the heavy fighting that accompanied the seizure of the South Dublin Union. His death sentence was commuted to penal servitude for life, and he was released under the 1917 amnesty.

Cosgrave quickly won a parliamentary by-election in Kilkenny City, and was unopposed in the 1918 general election. As treasurer of Sinn Féin, he was soon rearrested, but on release in 1919 became local government minister in the First Dáil, and did much to undermine the existing institutions.

He supported the 1921 Anglo-Irish Treaty and, after the deaths of Griffith and Collins, became chairman of the provisional government and then president of the executive council (i.e., prime minister) of the new Irish Free State. A quiet and undemonstrative leader, Cosgrave held this office until 1932; he also held for a time the portfolios in finance and defence, the latter after a threatened army mutiny in 1924.

By the time he was defeated by Eamon de Valera in 1932, Cosgrave had established a secure parliamentary democracy and had achieved in dominion status a cordial and almost complete independence from the United Kingdom. In opposition, he led Cumann na Gaedheal (as his party had become) until a 1933 merger produced Fine Gael (Tribe of Gaels), with Gen. Eoin O'Duffy as president of the new party.

O'Duffy had been dismissed as commissioner of police

by de Valera, and his Blueshirt movement briefly threatened the country's stability until he gave way to the level-headed Cosgrave who remained opposition leader until 1944. On resigning from the Dáil, Cosgrave became a member of the Irish Racing Board, and was its chairman for many years. He died in Dublin on 16 November 1965.

See
A plaque marks Cosgrave's birthplace.

EAMON DE VALERA
1882-1975
POLITICIAN

De Valera was born in New York on 14 October 1882. His Spanish father died in 1885, and he was sent to his grandmother's cottage at Bruree, Co. Limerick. He graduated from the Royal University in 1904, lectured in mathematics, and in 1910 married Sinead Flanagan, who had taught him Irish.

Baptised Edward, he became Eamon on joining the Gaelic League in 1908. He joined both the Irish Volunteers and the Irish Republican Brotherhood, and in the 1916 rising commanded the garrison at

The Dáil

Boland's Mills; his death sentence was commuted, and he

was released in 1917. Elected MP for East Clare, he quit the IRB, and succeeded Griffith as president of Sinn Féin in 1917. Interned in 1918, he escaped from Lincoln Jail to be elected president of the separatist Dáil Éireann.

In July 1921, a truce halted the War of Independence but de Valera rejected the Anglo-Irish Treaty negotiated by Griffith and Collins, criticising principally the oath of allegiance to the crown, and resigned the presidency. During the ensuing Civil War, he formed a rival government, but in May 1923 persuaded the Irish Republican Army to give up its unequal struggle against the Irish Free State. In 1926, de Valera broke with Sinn Féin to form Fianna Fáil (Warriors of Destiny). Successful in the 1932 election, he held power until defeated in 1948. The oath was removed in 1933, and in 1936 an External Relations Act largely abolished the crown's role. The IRA was proscribed, and in 1937 a new constitution reflected Catholic social policy as much as republicanism. 'Dev' became taoiseach or prime minister of the renamed Eire or Ireland whose neutrality he maintained in World War II.

Despite failing eyesight, he had two more periods in office, but two major objectives eluded him: an end to partition and revival of the Irish language. De Valera was elected president of Ireland in 1959, and served two seven-year terms. He died in Dublin on 29 August 1975.

Visit
Aras de Valera Museum, Bruree, Co. Limerick.

See
Statue in Ennis, Co. Clare.

HARRY FERGUSON
1884-1960
INVENTOR

Ferguson was born at Growell, near Hillsborough, Co. Down, on 4 November 1884. In 1902, he joined his brother Joe in a car and bicycle repair business in Belfast, and in 1904 began to race motor-cycles. In 1909, at Hillsborough, he made the first powered flight in Ireland, travelling 130 yd (118.5 m) in a monoplane he had built. He later drove racing cars, and helped to establish the famous Ulster Tourist Trophy races in 1928. Ferguson formed his own motor business in 1911, and during World War I began to sell tractors to Irish farmers accustomed to horse-drawn ploughs. With the revolutionary concept that tractor and plough should be designed as a unit, Ferguson began to register his own patents. The American tycoon Henry Ford offered him a job, but he preferred his independence and set up an American plant to make Ferguson ploughs. In 1926, the principal patent of the Ferguson system – hydraulic regulation of the working depth of the various implements linked to the tractor – was granted. In time, the system would change the face of agriculture, but commercial success proved elusive.

In 1938, Ferguson and Ford reached a 'gentlemen's agreement' by which the American could manufacture tractors for Ferguson to sell, and the deal was sealed only by a handshake. The tractor contributed enormously to wartime food production, but Ferguson's real hope was to raise living standards throughout the world. 'Agriculture,' he said in 1943, 'should have been the first industry to be modernised, not the last.' Ferguson's later years were clouded by a dispute with the Ford Motor Company, after Henry Ford's death. He won $9.25m compensation in 1952, but a 1953 merger with the Canadian Massey-Harris concern worked out unhappily for him, and he retired to Stow-on-the-Wold, in Gloucestershire.

His last ambition was to improve car safety through a four-wheel drive system and anti-lock braking, but he failed to make a commercial breakthrough. He suffered from insomnia and depression and, when he died from a drugs overdose on 25 October 1960, a coroner's jury returned an open verdict.

See
A blue plaque on the Ulster Bank, Donegall Square East, Belfast marks the site of Ferguson's show room.

MICHAEL COLLINS
1890-1922
REVOLUTIONARY

Collins was born near Sam's Cross, Clonakilty, Co. Cork, on 16 October 1890. He became a post office clerk in 1906. Sent to London, he learned Irish at Gaelic League classes and joined Sinn Féin. He later joined both the Irish Republican Brotherhood and the Irish Volunteers before returning to Ireland in January 1916, to avoid conscription in England.

G.P.O. Building, Dublin

During the Easter Rising, Collins fought in the General Post Office. In December 1916, he was released from internment and became a member of the IRB supreme council. When Eamon de Valera and other republicans were arrested in 1918, Collins eluded the police and began to build up a remarkable intelligence system. Elected MP for South Cork in 1918, 'the Big Fellow' became home minister in the First Dáil, but missed its opening; he was preparing de Valera's escape from Lincoln jail. He later became president of the IRB's supreme council.

In the ensuing guerrilla warfare, Collins' special squad systematically assassinated members of the 'G' division of the Dublin police, Dublin Castle's main source of intelligence; he had his own informants at detective headquarters. On 'Bloody Sunday', 21 November 1920, his men shot dead eleven British intelligence officers. In retaliation, British Black and Tans killed fourteen people at a football game. Collins' family home in Cork was burned out in April 1921.

A reluctant negotiator and signatory of the 1921 Anglo-Irish Treaty, Collins wrote 'early this morning I signed my death warrant'. He became chairman of the provisional government which preceded the Irish Free State, and Dublin Castle was surrendered to him. On the outbreak of the Civil War in June 1922, he took command of the forces loyal to the government.

On 22 August 1922, ten days after the death of Arthur Griffith he was ambushed and shot dead at Béal na mBláth, Co. Cork.

See

Memorials at Sam's Cross (4¼ miles/7 km WSW of Clonakilty); at Béal na mBláth (2 miles/3 km SW of Crookstown, Co. Cork); and at Leinster Lawn, Merrion Square, Dublin.

PEADAR O'DONNELL
1893-1986
TRADE UNIONIST AND POLITICAL WRITER

O'Donnell was born on a small farm near Dungloe, Co. Donegal, on 22 February 1893. He trained as a teacher in Dublin during 1911-13 and was influenced by the revolutionary ideas of James Larkin, James Connolly and Patrick Pearse. Returning to Donegal, he taught in the Innisfree and Aranmore islands, but later moved to Scotland, where he became active in the trade union movement, helping to improve the conditions of 'tatiehokers', the migrant Irish potato harvesters.

O'Donnell Cottage, Co. Donegal

In 1918 O'Donnell returned to Ireland as an organiser for the Irish Transport and General Workers' Union. During the War of Independence he led a brigade of the Irish Republican Army in Donegal. An opponent of the 1921 Anglo-Irish Treaty, he was in the Four Courts in Dublin when the Civil War broke out, and spent almost two years in prison before escaping from the Curragh. He later edited the republican journal *An Phoblacht*, engaging in a successful campaign against land annuities, but was eventually expelled from the IRA. His socialism also made him unpopular with right-wing Catholic groups.

O'Donnell's first novel, *Storm*, appeared in 1925, but it

was *Islanders* (1928) which established his literary reputation. In the novel a woman starves herself so that her children can eat. In *Adrigoole* (1929), based on actual events, a mother and child starve to death while the husband is in prison. O'Donnell's deeply realistic novels centre on the poverty of farming and fishing families in the West of Ireland, and are often didactic in tone. Of his later novels, the best is *The Big Windows* (1955), in which an islandwoman misses the open sky when marriage takes her to a narrow glen. His last book, *Proud Island*, appeared in 1975.

O'Donnell also wrote three autobiographical books: *The Gates Flew Open* (1932), about prison life, *Salud!* (1937), recalling the Spanish Civil War, and *There Will Be Another Day* (1963). In 1940 he and Sean O'Faolain founded *The Bell*, which O'Donnell edited from 1946 until its closure in 1954. The magazine provided an important outlet for new Irish writing, as well as taking a liberal stance on matters such as censorship and the 1951 Mother and Child controversy. In later years O'Donnell espoused such causes as nuclear disarmament and agitation against the Vietnam war. He died in Dublin on 13 May 1986.

SEAN LEMASS
1899-1971
POLITICIAN

Lemass was born at Ballybrack, Co. Dublin, on 15 July 1899. His father was a draper in Capel Street, Dublin, and an active supporter of the Irish parliamentary party. Lemass was fifteen when he joined the Irish Volunteers. When the 1916 rising began, he joined the occupiers of the General Post Office; because of his youth, he was released soon after the surrender. Active in the War of Independence, he was arrested in 1920 and interned for a year at Ballykinler, Co. Down.

Opposed to the 1921 Anglo-Irish Treaty, Lemass was second-in-command when anti-Treaty members of the Irish Republican Army occupied the Four Courts in Dublin in 1922. After the garrison surrendered, he escaped to fight in the Civil War, but was later captured and interned. When Eamon de Valera formed the Fianna Fáil party in 1926, Lemass became its secretary and creator of a formidable political machine. In 1932, he became minister for industry and commerce in the first Fianna Fáil government; apart from brief periods in opposition, he held this post until 1959.

During the 1930s, Lemass favoured protective tariffs; he set up large public enterprises such as Aer Lingus and the peat-exploiting Bord na Móna. In 1959, he succeeded de Valera as taoiseach, and pursued a vigorous policy of economic expansion, encouraging foreign investors. In 1965, he concluded a free trade agreement with the United Kingdom, in preparation for entry into the European Economic Community, and by his pragmatism turned an inward-looking country into one with new horizons and self-confidence. He courageously visited the prime minister of Northern Ireland, Capt. Terence O'Neill, in an attempt to improve relations between the two parts of Ireland.

Lemass resigned from office in 1966, and left the Dáil in 1969. He joined the board of many Irish companies, indulging a taste for business that had been suppressed during his political career, save that he managed his country like an ambitious entrepreneur. He died in Dublin on 11 May 1971.

MICHEÁL MAC LIAMMÓIR
1899-1978
ACTOR AND AUTHOR

Mac Liammóir was born in London on 25 October 1899. His real name was Alfred Willmore, and as a child actor he took a number of West End roles. He went on to study art, and later designed for Edward Martyn's Irish Theatre and the Dublin Drama League. He spent several years painting in Europe before joining Anew McMaster's touring company, performing Shakespeare by oil lamp on makeshift Irish stages.

Gate Theatre, Dublin

Mac Liammóir had joined the Gaelic League in London, and was a fluent Irish speaker. In August 1928, he directed his own play, *Diarmuid agus Gráinne*, at the opening of the Taibhdearc na Gaillimhe, a government-subsidised Gaelic theatre in Galway. Two months later, he and Hilton Edwards, an Englishman who was to be his lifelong associate, opened the Gate Theatre in Dublin. They began in an annexe of the Abbey Theatre, staging *Peer Gynt* with a cast of 48 before a capacity audience of 102.

In 1930, the Gate found a larger permanent home in Parnell Square, and a generous benefactor in the 6th Earl of Longford. The Abbey's staple was now kitchen comedy, and the Gate set new standards of professionalism in a wide range of international drama. Mac Liammóir himself had every theatrical talent: he was actor, director, playwright, designer of sets and costumes, and able to translate from several languages.

In 1947 he starred in his own *Ill Met by Moonlight* in London, then made his New York debut in *John Bull's Other Island* in 1948. He played Iago in Orson Welles' *Othello* (1949), and published a diary of the film, *Put Money in Thy Purse* (1952). Other memoirs included *All for Hecuba* (1946), *Each Actor on His Ass* (1960) and *Enter a Goldfish* (1977).

His 1932 Hamlet was possibly his finest performance, but his greatest success came in 1960, with a one-man show, *The Importance of Being Oscar*, which captivated audiences throughout the world. In 1975, his last stage performance was his 1384th as Oscar Wilde, appropriately at the Gate. He died in Dublin on 6 March 1978.

See
Plaque at 4 Harcourt Terrace, Dublin, the Regency house he shared with Edwards (1903-1982).

TERENCE O'NEILL
1914-1990
POLITICIAN

O'Neill, a member of a family descended from the Uí Néill high kings of Ireland, was born in London on 10 September 1914. His father was the first Member of Parliament to be killed in World War I. Educated at Eton, O'Neill had various jobs before becoming aide-de-camp to the Governor of South Australia. In World War II, he served with the Irish Guards.

After the war, O'Neill moved to Northern Ireland, hoping to make a career in politics. In 1946 he became Unionist MP for the Bannside constituency at Stormont, and was unopposed there until 1969, when he narrowly defeated Ian Paisley (*see page 117*). He held minor posts before becoming Minister of Home Affairs in 1956. Later in the year he became Minister of Finance and in 1963 succeeded Viscount Brookeborough as Prime Minister.

Stormont, Belfast

The Unionists, essentially a Protestant party, had held power since 1921. O'Neill believed that new attitudes and policies were needed in Northern Ireland, and that the Roman Catholic minority must be encouraged to play a full part in Ulster life. He spoke of building bridges in the community, and in 1965 signalled a friendlier relationship with the Irish Republic by initiating meetings with the Taoiseach, Sean Lemass (*see page 109*). While many people welcomed O'Neill's more liberal policies, he faced opposition within his own party and from Paisley, who always had greater rapport with working class Protestants than the aristocratic O'Neill.

O'Neill's position was made more difficult by republican celebrations marking the fiftieth anniversary of the 1916 Easter Rising and by the emergence of a Protestant terrorist organisation, the Ulster Volunteer Force. On 5 October 1968, police in Londonderry batoned civil rights demonstrators who defied a government ban on their march. With the British government pressing for reform, O'Neill announced a programme which dealt particularly with grievances in local government.

In December 1968, O'Neill broadcast an appeal for peace, posing the question: 'What kind of Ulster do you want?' It was well received by moderate opinion, but there was renewed civil unrest in 1969. After an inconclusive general election, O'Neill gave up the struggle and resigned. He entered the British House of Lords as Lord O'Neill of the Maine, and died at Lymington, Hampshire, on 12 June 1990.

CONOR CRUISE O'BRIEN
1917-
WRITER AND POLITICIAN

O'Brien was born in Dublin on 3 November 1917. His father, a journalist who died when his son was ten, and his mother both came from families active in Irish nationalist politics. He was educated at Sandford Park and Trinity College, Dublin, and in 1942 entered the Irish Civil Service, moving to the External Affairs department in 1944.

In 1950 he became managing director of the new Irish News Agency, a government-sponsored body which publicised the case for a united Ireland. He had begun writing for literary magazines, under the pen-name Donat O'Donnell, and a collection on modern Catholic authors, *Maria Cross*, was published in 1952. His doctorate on Charles Stewart Parnell (*see page 73*), was published as *Parnell and His Party* (1957).

In 1956, following a short spell in Paris, O'Brien moved to his department's United Nations section, and in 1961 he was seconded to head a UN peace-keeping mission in the Congo. O'Brien's decision to use troops against the secessionist province of Katanga led to his recall to New York. He resigned from the UN and from External Affairs, and later defended his controversial conduct in *To Katanga and Back* (1962), returning to the subject in his play *Murderous Angels* (1968).

O'Brien embarked on an academic career, becoming vice-chancellor of the University of Ghana in 1962, then Albert Schweitzer Professor of Humanities at New York University in 1965. He returned to Ireland in 1969, winning a Dáil seat for the Irish Labour Party. Later, as Minister for Posts and Telegraphs in the 1973-77 coalition government, he created controversy by banning broadcasts by IRA spokesmen. O'Brien knew Northern Ireland better than most southern politicians, and often courted unpopularity by sympathising with northern Protestants' resistance to a united Ireland.

He lost his Dáil seat in 1977, but won a university seat in the Senate. He resigned in 1978 to become editor-in-chief of *The Observer*, the British Sunday newspaper, until 1981. He has continued to mix academic and journalistic work, and was active for a time in one of Northern Ireland's smaller Unionist parties. He published *The Great Melody*, a biography of Edmund Burke (*see page 33*) in 1992, and *Ancestral Voices*, an examination of Catholic nationalism, in 1994.

CHARLES HAUGHEY
1925-2006
POLITICIAN

Haughey was born on 16 September 1925 in Castlebar, Co. Mayo. His father served with the IRA during the War of Independence and had become a commandant in the new Irish Army. Haughey studied commerce at University College, Dublin, and in 1950 formed an accountancy firm. He had joined the Fianna Fáil party, and in 1951 he married Maureen Lemass, daughter of the future Taoiseach Sean Lemass (*see page 109*).

Haughey entered parliament in 1957, and in 1961 became Minister for Justice. Among his reforms were the abolition of the death penalty, apart from a few crimes such as murder of policemen, and a Bill to give inheritance rights to widows and children. He introduced military courts which helped to end a five-year IRA campaign of violence in Northern Ireland. Later, as Minister for Finance, he devised a scheme of tax exemption which encouraged writers and artists to settle in Ireland.

In August 1969, serious rioting broke out in Northern Ireland. Haughey was put in charge of a £100,000 relief fund, voted by the Dáil, from which money was later used to buy arms for the defence of Catholic areas in Northern Ireland, where the IRA was again active. In 1970 Haughey was dismissed from office and charged with conspiracy to import arms illegally, but was acquitted.

He gradually rebuilt his political career, and in 1977 became Minister for Health and Social Welfare. His Family Planning Act legalised the sale of contraceptives for married couples. When Jack Lynch retired in 1979, the charismatic Haughey was elected Taoiseach but was defeated in the 1981 general election. He regained office in 1982, but his government soon collapsed, following scandals over the tapping of political journalists' telephones and the arrest of a murder suspect in the attorney general's apartment.

Haughey regained power in 1987, but was forced into coalition in 1989, and a series of financial scandals in the beef and sugar industries and in property development, from which Haughey's friends had benefited financially, led to his resignation in 1992. Haughey's extravagant life style had always aroused speculation, and succeeding years uncovered new scandals, not least that he had once received a gift of £1.3m from a Dublin businessman.

Charles Haughey died on 13 June 2006, and was given a state funeral. The Taoiseach Bertie Ahern said: "Charles Haughey brought to the office of Taoiseach a wide array of talents and skills, perhaps unmatched in the modern era."

IAN PAISLEY
1926-
CLERIC AND POLITICIAN

Paisley was born in Armagh on 6 April 1926. Two years later his father, a Baptist pastor, moved to Ballymena, Co. Antrim. Following a row in the church, he set up a gospel tabernacle in 1933. On leaving school, Ian Paisley trained at an evangelical college in Wales, and then at a Reformed Presbyterian seminary in Belfast. Ordained by his father in 1946, he became pastor of a mission church in Belfast.

Always an effective preacher with fundamentalist views, Paisley soon had a reputation as a virulent critic of the Roman Catholic Church. In 1951, he took advantage of a dispute in a Presbyterian church in Crossgar, Co. Down, to form the Free Presbyterian Church of Ulster. Paisley became Moderator of the new Church, creating new congregations throughout Northern Ireland and eventually outside it.

During the 1950s Paisley was involved in anti-Catholic groups such as the National Union of Protestants and Ulster Protestant Action, and he has even travelled to the Vatican to oppose ecumenism. In 1966 he was found guilty of illegal assembly when he protested against 'Romanising tendencies' in the Presbyterian Church, and served a prison sentence rather than pay a fine.

When Terence O'Neill (*see page 112*) invited Sean Lemass (*see page 109*) to Belfast in 1965, Paisley immediately registered a protest. Placards saying 'O'Neill must go' greeted the Prime Minister wherever he spoke. Paisley polled strongly in O'Neill's Bannside constituency in the 1969 general election, and won the seat comfortably in April 1970 after O'Neill retired to the House of Lords. Two months later he became MP for North Antrim at Westminster, and in 1979 he was elected to the European Parliament.

Paisley's Protestant Unionist Party developed into the Democratic Unionist Party, which he has led since 1971, and he has been joined by other DUP members at Westminster and in the different Ulster assemblies of recent years. He now shows more devotion to democratic processes and less to the public rallies and street demonstrations which once brought him notoriety. His political achievements have been negative rather than positive, but for many, inside and outside the province, he remains the true voice of Ulster Protestantism.

RICHARD HARRIS
1930-2002
ACTOR

Harris was born in Limerick on 1 October 1930. On leaving Crescent College, where his principal interest had been rugby football, he worked in the family flour mill. He already had a reputation for wildness but, on contracting tuberculosis, he thought seriously about his future, and decided to become a professional actor. He was accepted at the London Academy of Music and Dramatic Art.

In 1956 he appeared in Brendan Behan's *The Quare Fellow* at Joan Littlewood's Theatre Workshop at Stratford East. When he was seen by the American playwright Arthur Miller, it led to a part in the London production of Miller's *A View from the Bridge*. He began to get small film parts, returning to Ireland for *Shake Hands with the Devil* (1959), with James Cagney, and *A Terrible Beauty* (1960), with Robert Mitchum. On stage he was well cast as *The Ginger Man* (1959), and played the rumbustious hero of J.P. Donleavy's play, first in London and then in Dublin, where the play was criticised as anti-Catholic and withdrawn after three nights.

Harris's developing film career brought work with Gregory Peck in *The Guns of Navarone* (1961) and Marlon Brando in

Mutiny on the Bounty (1962), but it was a British film, Lindsay Anderson's *This Sporting Life* (1963) which demonstrated both his acting skill and his star quality. He was ideally cast as Frank Machin, an aggressive rugby league footballer.

Harris quickly established himself in Hollywood with a number of major roles. The majority of his best films capitalised on his strong physical presence, notably *Major Dundee* (1964), *The Heroes of Telemark* (1965), *The Molly Maguires* (1969) and *A Man Called Horse* (1970). However, he also played Cain in *The Bible* (1966), the title role in *Cromwell* (1970), and King Richard in *Robin and Marian* (1976). Following his role as King Arthur in the musical film *Camelot* (1967) he had some success as a singer, notably with his recording of 'MacArthur Park' (1968).

His hard-drinking life frequently took its toll on his health and on his marriages. Of his later action films *The Wild Geese* (1977) is probably the best of a poor lot. However, he was still able to win an Oscar nomination when he returned to Ireland to play Bull McCabe in *The Field* (1990). In later years Harris's roles included a Roman emperor in *Gladiator* (2000) but he may be best remembered now for having played Professor Dumbledore in the first two 'Harry Potter' film adaptations. He died on 26 October 2002.

GAY BYRNE
1934-
BROADCASTER

Byrne was born in Dublin on 5 August 1934. His father, formerly a soldier in the British Army, was skipper of a Guinness barge on the River Liffey. On leaving Synge Street Christian Brothers School Byrne worked for an insurance company. However, he had early decided on a career in broadcasting, and his persistence began to produce modest jobs – reading commercials, commentating at stock-car races, compering stage shows – and he became radio producer with an advertising agency. Eventually Radio Éireann offered him part-time employment as newsreader and continuity announcer.

Byrne had always hoped to emulate the Irish broadcaster Éamonn Andrews, a former neighbour who had gained success in England. He persuaded Granada Television to give him a trial as newscaster and reporter, and divided his week between Manchester and Dublin. When the Irish television service was established in 1961, Byrne was well equipped to exploit new opportunities. In 1962 he introduced *The Late Late Show*, a new weekend chat show destined to set records for longevity.

Byrne had moved to London to work for the new BBC2 channel, and in 1966 he was replaced on *The Late Late Show*. A year later he accepted an invitation to return, on condition that he could also produce the show. He became associated with a succession of popular TV programmes, and in 1972 launched *The Gay Byrne Show*, a morning radio programme which consolidated his unique position in Irish broadcasting.

Like other chat shows, *The Late Late Show* relies on its celebrity guests, but its continuing importance has rested in modernising Irish society by opening up every controversial issue to debate. Byrne's gift has been to make the Irish talk to each other on subjects, not least sexual mores or the shortcomings of the Roman Catholic Church, where there would once have been complete reticence. The studio audience is an essential element. Byrne retired from *The Late Late Show* in 1999.

In addition to writing regularly for newspapers and magazines, Byrne is the author of *To Whom It Concerns* (1972), marking the early years of his TV show, and co-author of his anecdotal autobiography, *The Time of My Life* (1989). He has now begun to reduce his commitments, but it is unlikely that any future Irish broadcaster will be so influential.

TONY O'REILLY
1936-
ENTREPRENEUR

O'Reilly was born in Dublin on 7 May 1936. He was the son of a civil servant who had left his wife and four children, and lived something of a double life. O'Reilly himself would marry twice, divorcing his Australian wife and later marrying the daughter of a Greek ship owner.

He was educated at Belvedere College, where he excelled at several sports, and at University College, Dublin, where he studied law. On the rugby football field, he became a strong and speedy wing three-quarter, and in 1955 he won the first of 29 caps playing for Ireland. In the same year he was picked for the prestigious Lions' tour of South Africa. He also toured with the Lions in 1959, setting a try-scoring record in Australia and New Zealand.

On graduating in 1958, O'Reilly became a management consultant. He worked in England, before returning to Ireland, where in 1962 he was appointed general manager of An Bord Bainne, the new Irish Dairy Board. His success in marketing Irish butter under the Kerrygold brand name set him off on a spectacular business career.

In 1966 he was persuaded to become managing director of the semi-state Irish Sugar Company, whose subsidiary Erin Foods was losing money. O'Reilly's solution was to negotiate a deal with the American food giant, Heinz, an association which led to his appointment as managing director of Heinz U.K. in 1969. Two years later he moved to the Heinz headquarters in Pittsburgh, and in 1973 he became president and chief operating officer of the company. He became chief executive in 1979, and later the first chairman not from the Heinz family. A noted raconteur, he once defined the secret of his success in America as 'Look Irish, think Yiddish, dress British'.

O'Reilly is Ireland's richest businessman. His contract

with Heinz allowed him to develop other business interests, which have brought him regularly to Ireland. They include the Fitzwilton holding company, the *Irish Independent* and other newspapers, and the Waterford Wedgwood glass and china company, which he saved from closure. He was also a founder of the Ireland Fund, using his charismatic charm to raise money for projects to bring peace in Ireland.

JOHN HUME
1937-
POLITICIAN

Hume was born in Londonderry on 18 January 1937. Educated at St Columb's College, Hume went to St Patrick's College, Maynooth, intending to become a priest, but later recognised a loss of vocation. On graduating in 1958, he became a schoolmaster, and soon returned to his old school.

Hume's initial interests were less in politics than in community development. He helped to found the Derry Credit Union in 1960, and in 1965 became first chairman of the Derry Housing Association. Drawn into the civil rights movement, he became MP for Foyle at Stormont in 1969. In 1970 he became a founder of the Social Democratic and Labour Party, which aspired to the peaceful reunification of Ireland.

Ulster was already in the grip of sectarian violence. In August 1969, Hume had been unable to prevent serious rioting in Derry, and the disorder had spread. In 1972 the British Government suspended the Stormont parliament, which the SDLP had boycotted after the introduction of internment. In Derry, thirteen Roman Catholics had been shot dead by the Paratroop Regiment on 'Bloody Sunday'. The illegal Irish Republican Army was a growing challenge, not merely to the government but to constitutional politicians such as Hume.

When a new Northern Ireland Assembly was elected in

1973, he became Minister of Commerce in a power-sharing executive. A general strike of Protestant workers ended the experiment in 1974. They objected to a proposed cross-border Council of Ireland as an infringement on British sovereignty. Hume has long argued that an 'Irish dimension' is necessary in any political settlement of Northern Ireland's problems.

He was elected to the European Parliament in 1979, and soon replaced Gerry Fitt as SDLP leader. He entered Westminster as MP for Foyle in 1983. In 1988 Hume initiated talks with Gerry Adams, leader of Sinn Féin, the IRA's political wing. It was the beginning of a long sequence of negotiations which eventually led to the 1998 Good Friday agreement, providing for a new Northern Ireland Assembly with a power-sharing executive and for cross-border bodies. After the agreement was endorsed in referendums held in both parts of Ireland, Hume and the Unionist leader, David Trimble, were jointly awarded the Nobel Peace Prize.

MARY ROBINSON
1944-
BARRISTER AND POLITICIAN

Mary Robinson (née Bourke) was born in Ballina, Co. Mayo, on 21 May 1944. Her parents were both doctors, but there was also a legal tradition in the family. On leaving Mount Anville School, a convent boarding school in Dublin, she spent a year in a Paris finishing school. At the time, the Roman Catholic Church banned its members from sending their children to Trinity College, Dublin, but the ban was waived for her, and in 1963 she entered TCD to read law. She was later to marry, in 1970, a Protestant and fellow law graduate, Nick Robinson.

Graduating with first class honours in 1967, she won a scholarship to Harvard University. It proved a formative year, as she witnessed how the Vietnam war and the civil rights movement were forcing Americans to re-examine their country. Returning to Ireland, she practised at the bar, and in 1969 was appointed to a professorship in constitutional and criminal law at TCD. In the same year, she became the first Roman Catholic that TCD graduates elected to the Irish Senate. In 1976 she joined the Irish Labour Party, but resigned over the 1985 Anglo-Irish Agreement, which she rightly believed would polarise the two communities in Northern Ireland.

Mary Robinson had by now become a trenchant critic of the shortcomings of Irish society. She was active in human rights cases in both Irish and European courts, many of them touching on the place of women in Irish society, and was an authority on European Community law. On the whole, she enjoyed greater success in the courts than in parliament, where she faced resistance to her efforts to liberalise Irish law on such matters as contraception and divorce. She twice failed to win a seat in the Dáil, and in 1989 retired from the Senate to concentrate on her busy legal career.

In 1990 the Labour Party invited her to stand for the Irish presidency, and a well-organised campaign took her to victory. At her inauguration Robinson spoke of a new Ireland, which would be open, tolerant, inclusive and pluralist. In the years that followed, she significantly raised the profile of the presidency in Ireland and abroad. In 1997 she was appointed United Nations high commissioner for refugees.

GEORGE BEST
1946-2005
FOOTBALLER

Best was born in Belfast on 22 May 1946. His father, who worked in the shipyard, had been an amateur footballer and his mother was a keen hockey player. An early photograph shows Best at fourteen months with a ball at his feet. As a boy, he was obsessed with soccer, and received valuable coaching from his father. He played for different school and boys' club teams in the hope that he would be spotted by one of the scouts who followed their games.

At fifteen, he was about to become an apprentice printer when Bob Bishop, Manchester United's scout in Belfast, offered him a trial in England. Although Best was small and light, Bishop had no doubt that he could defeat stronger opponents. His telegram to Manchester said: 'I have found a genius'.

Gable wall mural, Belfast

Best was initially homesick and returned to Belfast, but he was persuaded to go back to the club, where Sir Matt Busby had rebuilt a winning team after a disastrous air crash at Munich in 1958.

Best was only seventeen when he made his debut with the first team. He soon became a favourite with the supporters at Manchester's Old Trafford stadium, who admired his outstanding ball control and his gift for goal-scoring. The cheeky new 'Busby Babe' was both an entertainer and a footballer. With other great players such as Bobby Charlton and Denis Law, Best helped his team to English League championships in 1965 and 1967, and to winning the European Cup in 1968, when he was named European Player of the Year. Surprisingly, United never reached the final of the Football Association Cup, but Best did set a record by scoring six goals in a 1970 tie. He also played 37 times for Northern Ireland.

As Manchester United's fortunes waned, so did Best's footballing skills, and his life became less disciplined. He drank heavily, and his affairs and quick-tempered brawls increased the media pressure. On leaving Manchester in 1974 Best played for a number of other clubs, including Fulham and the Los Angeles Aztecs, but he never recaptured the consistent magic that had made him perhaps the greatest footballer of his generation. His life was appropriately summed up in the title of his 1990 autobiography, *The Good, the Bad and the Bubbly*. He died on 25 November 2005. His funeral procession to Stormont Parliament Buildings was lined by thousands of fans. Best has a lasting memorial in the renamed George Best Belfast City Airport and the memories of those who love football.

U2
1978-
MUSICIANS

In 1976 a group of teenagers at Mount Temple Comprehensive School in Dublin formed a band called Feedback. Seven original members came down to five, and they changed their name to The Hype. Then there were four, and in 1978 they became known as U2. They were still teenagers, but were destined to become one of the world's most successful rock bands.

Larry Mullen, the drummer, was the youngest (born 1 October 1961). David Evans (8 August 1961) played guitar, and became known as The Edge. Paul Hewson (10 May 1960), was the singer, and became known as Bono. The oldest member, guitarist Adam Clayton (13 March 1960), acted as the band's manager.

Popular music in Ireland had for some years been dominated by showbands. However, rock bands such as the Boomtown Rats, Horslips and Thin Lizzie had begun to capture a new and younger audience in Ireland and abroad. In 1978, The Hype won a talent competition in Limerick. Soon afterwards, having become U2, the four musicians found a manager, Paul McGuinness, who recognised their potential.

The band's first record, *U2-3*, was well received when it was released in Ireland in 1979, and in 1980 U2 signed a contract with Island Records, which released their debut album *Boy*. They began to tour more widely in Europe and America, promoting their albums *October* (1981) and *War* (1983). A video of their 1983 concert at Denver, Colorado, *U2 Live at Red Rocks: Under a Blood Red Sky*, paved the way for a successful Australian tour in 1984.

Other album successes were *The Unforgettable Fire* (1984), which drew its title from paintings by Japanese survivors of the 1945 atomic bombs, and *The Joshua Tree* (1987). *Rattle and Hum* (1988) had a mixed reception, but the band's *Achtung Baby* (1991), bleaker than much of their earlier work, was a worldwide hit. On tour, performing in the largest stadiums throughout the world, their staging has become increasingly spectacular.

U2 have regularly shown a strong social conscience, performing for such causes as famine relief and Amnesty International. A 'Self Aid' festival in Dublin in 1986 raised money to tackle Ireland's unemployment problems. More recently Bono has added his voice to the campaign to relieve Third World debt.

Index